MODERN JEWELRY FROM MODULAR PARTS

MODERN JEWELRY FROM MODULAR PARTS

EASY PROJECTS USING READYMADE COMPONENTS

SOUTH CAMPUS

● Marthe Le Van

LARK BOOKS
A Division of Sterling Publishing Co., Inc.
New York / London

EDITOR:
LARRY SHEA
ART DIRECTOR:
MEGAN KIRBY
COVER DESIGNER:
CINDY LA BREACHT
EDITORIAL ASSISTANCE:
MARK BLOOM, CASSIE MOORE,
JULIE HALE, DAWN DILLINGHAM
ASSOCIATE ART DIRECTOR:
SHANNON YOKELY
ART ASSISTANT:
TRAVIS PRICE
PRODUCTION ASSISTANT:
JEFF HAMILTON
PROJECT PHOTOGRAPHER:
STEWART O'SHIELDS
ILLUSTRATOR: ORRIN LUNDGREN
PROOFREADER: VAL ANDERSON

Library of Congress Cataloging-in-Publication Data

Le Van, Marthe.
   Modern jewelry from modular parts : easy projects using readymade components / Marthe Le Van.
          p. cm.
   Includes bibliographical references and index.
   ISBN-13: 978-1-60059-047-4 (hc-plc with jacket : alk. paper)
   ISBN-10: 1-60059-047-0 (hc-plc with jacket : alk. paper)
1. Jewelry making. I. Title.
TT212.L495 2007
745.594'2--dc22

                                                    2007018663

10 9 8 7 6 5 4 3 2 1

First Edition

Published by Lark Books, A Division of
Sterling Publishing Co., Inc.
387 Park Avenue South, New York, N.Y. 10016

Text © 2007, Lark Books
Photography © 2007, Lark Books unless otherwise specified
Illustrations © 2007, Lark Books

Distributed in Canada by Sterling Publishing,
c/o Canadian Manda Group, 165 Dufferin Street
Toronto, Ontario, Canada M6K 3H6

Distributed in the United Kingdom by GMC Distribution Services,
Castle Place, 166 High Street, Lewes, East Sussex, England BN7 1XU

Distributed in Australia by Capricorn Link (Australia) Pty Ltd.,
P.O. Box 704, Windsor, NSW 2756 Australia

If you have questions or comments about this book, please contact:
Lark Books, 67 Broadway, Asheville, NC 28801, (828) 253-0467

Manufactured in China

ISBN 13: 978-1-60059-047-4
ISBN 10: 1-60059-047-0

For information about custom editions, special sales, premium and corporate purchases, please contact Sterling Special Sales Department at 800-805-5489 or specialsales@sterlingpub.com.

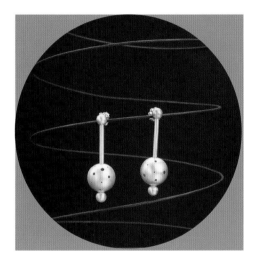

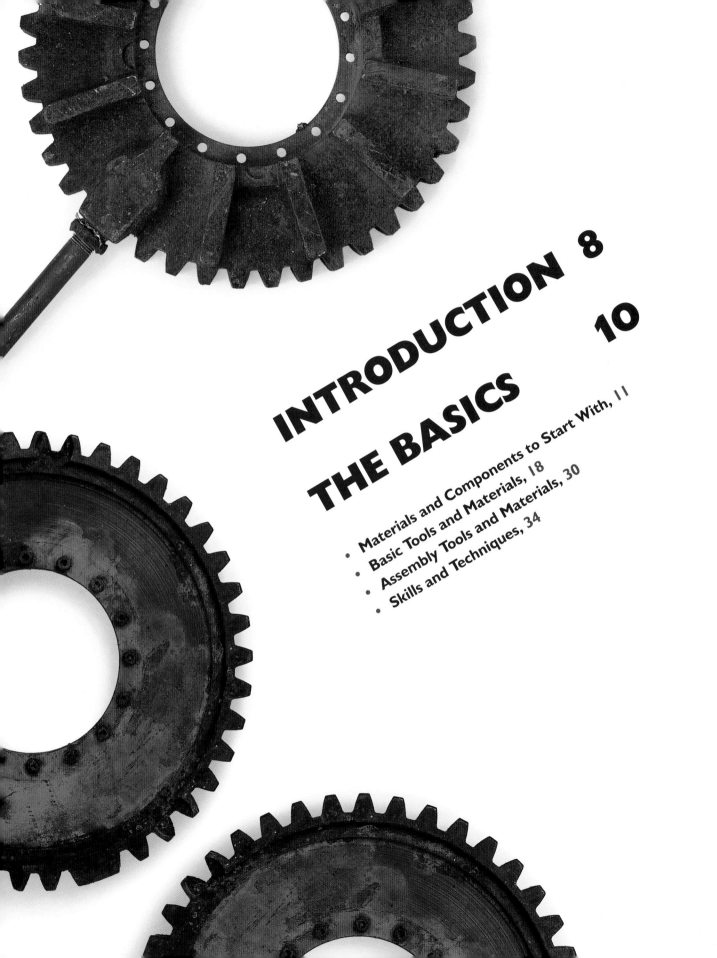

INTRODUCTION 8

THE BASICS 10

THE PROJECTS 42

INTRODUCTION

No matter what the subject, when you're dealing with the essentials of something, you could say you're getting down to its "nuts and bolts." In jewelry making, such basic elements would include those simple building blocks that are part of the foundations of the craft—jump rings, sheet metal, silver wire, pin backs, and other manufactured elements.

When you make metal jewelry with the modular techniques you'll learn in this book, you'll discover that this is a fast and easy way to use basic readymade components—and sometimes even actual nuts and bolts—in sophisticated and stylish designs. These pieces of jewelry start out as manufactured materials such as metal tubes, rods, and wire; commercial hardware and materials; and jewelry-making findings and components. How do you turn these common elements into uncommon jewelry? First,

you employ some simple techniques like sawing, cutting, filing, and drilling. Then, to assemble your components, you use some very easy methods (like connecting with jump rings), and others that take a bit more practice (like soldering and riveting). The Basics section that follows will explain the tools, materials, and techniques you need to make all the projects in the book.

Learning to create metal jewelry with modular techniques opens up a world of possibilities. Like the talented designers in this book, you could be browsing through a jewelry-supply catalog, or walking in a hardware store, and then start to imagine how objects you see could be combined into a creative jewelry design. With the easy techniques available, it might not be long before you've turned your idea into a striking piece of modern jewelry.

THE BASICS

When you make jewelry from modular parts, you start with a variety of manufactured materials, and then build them up and put them together to make something new and creative. In this section of the book, we're going to build up and put together all the basic knowledge you need for creating the projects that follow. I'll start with the building blocks of materials you can use when creating jewelry out of modular parts, and then go on to the essential tools, assembly processes, and special techniques you need to know about.

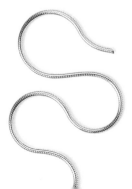

MATERIALS AND COMPONENTS TO START WITH

The materials that are the starting point for your modular pieces can be found in jewelry-supply catalogs, hardware stores, or—if you're really being creative—just about anywhere. Beginning with manufactured materials cuts down on some of the steps required to produce a piece of jewelry, but fortunately doesn't lessen the creativity needed to design and make attractive pieces.

● **LOEBER + LOOK**
Reed Brooch, 2006
3.3 x 4.8 x 0.6 cm
Sterling silver wire; hand cut, hand forged, soldered
Photo by Ralph Gabriner

Ferrous sheet metal, rods, and wire

Metal Types

All of the materials and components that follow in this section are available in different metals. Your choice of a type of metal may be guided by availability, price, color, or how easy it is to work with.

Metals are classified into two groups, ferrous and nonferrous. Ferrous metals either are iron or contain iron while nonferrous metals have no iron content. Nonferrous metals, such as silver and gold, are the ones most commonly used to make jewelry.

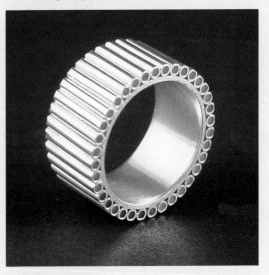

● **JENNY WINDLER**
Tube Ring, 2004
2.2 x 2.2 x 1.1 cm
Sterling silver, sterling silver tubing; hand cut, soldered
Photo by artist

11

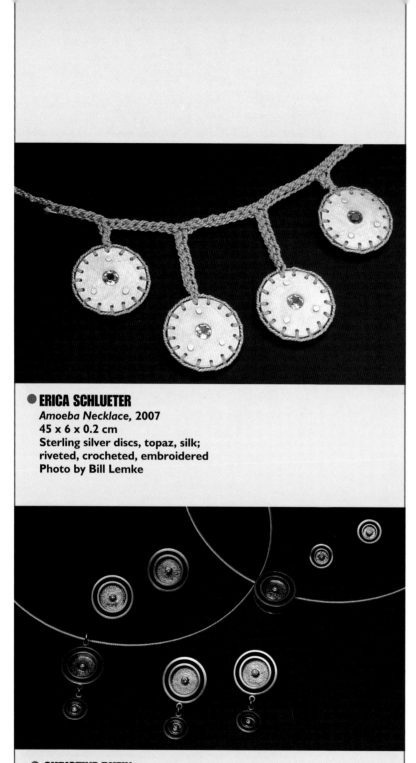

● **ERICA SCHLUETER**
Amoeba Necklace, 2007
45 x 6 x 0.2 cm
Sterling silver discs, topaz, silk;
riveted, crocheted, embroidered
Photo by Bill Lemke

● **CHRISTINE DHEIN**
Concentric Circle Collection, 2000
2.5 x 2.5 x 0.4 cm
24-karat gold, sterling silver,
rubber, diamonds; cast, kum boo,
hand finished, tube set
Photo by Don Felton

Silver is a beautiful and durable material, and sterling silver is the standard silver for jewelry. Sterling silver isn't pure silver; to increase pure silver's strength, it's combined with another metal or metals to make an alloy. The most common metal used is copper. The composition of sterling silver is 92.5 percent silver and 7.5 percent copper.

Like pure silver, pure **gold** is much too soft for most jewelry making, so it's usually mixed with other metals to make it more stable and versatile. The measuring scale in the United States for indicating the purity of gold is the karat, and the higher the percentage of pure gold the higher the karat. Metals mixed with pure gold can change the color of the gold, resulting in different shades of yellow, white, pink, and even green gold.

Copper is a pure metal that works well for both cold and hot jewelry-making techniques. Initially bright reddish brown in color, copper can also acquire rich green and brick red patinas through chemical or heat treatments. Copper is highly malleable, making it easy to work, and relatively low in cost.

Aluminum, like copper, is a pure nonferrous metal. With a highly reflective grayish-white color, aluminum is also lightweight (about one-third as heavy as copper or steel). Soft and malleable, aluminum is extremely easy to form, machine, and cast. Anodized aluminum is coated with a protective or decorative film and sold in a range of brilliant colors.

Brass is an alloy of copper and zinc valued for its golden color, hardness, and workability. Color

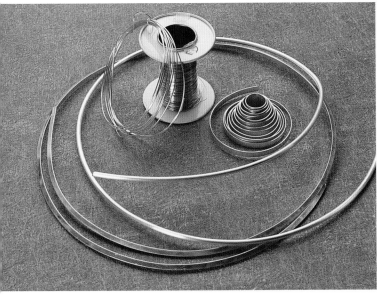

Wire in various metals and gauges

An assortment of metal tubing

variations of brass are the result of slightly different proportions of copper and zinc. It's more brittle than copper, harder to cut, and requires heating—also known as annealing—to stay soft during repeated hammering.

Steel is the common name for a family of iron alloys usually made from iron ore, coal, and limestone. Standard steels are classified into three major groups: carbon steels, alloy steels, and stainless steel. Stainless steel is a broad term for a group of corrosion-resistant steels that contain chromium. Stainless doesn't mean these alloys will never stain or corrode, but they will stain less than steels that don't contain chromium.

Other metals used in jewelry making that may be worth seeking out for their particular color or properties include **bronze** (an alloy of copper and tin and sometimes other elements), **nickel silver**, **niobium**, **pewter**, and **titanium**.

Wires and Rods

Metal wire is manufactured with many different profiles and in many different thicknesses. Round wire is most common, and you can also find half round, square, triangular, and more. Pre-patterned wires are available, and they can add an interesting element to a design. The thickness of wire is measured using the gauge system. Gauge numbers inversely specify the material's thickness—the thinner the metal, the higher its gauge number. (You can find a standard gauge measurement chart on page 123.) Precious metal wires are cut to the length ordered and priced by weight. Base metal wires, which are less expensive, are usually sold in predetermined lengths on a spool or in a coil. Metal rod is similar to wire, but rod is measured incrementally in millimeters of diameter rather than gauge, and is available in larger sizes.

When choosing wires or rods to use, you don't have to limit yourself to standard sizes or only shop from jewelry suppliers. One designer in the project section of this book was inspired in her piece to use steel guitar strings for their interesting texture.

Tubing

Tubing is a hollow metal cylinder. It's manufactured and sold with different wall thicknesses and diameters. Both of these measurements are given in millimeters rather than gauge. A tube has two diameters. One is measured outside the tube wall (the outside diameter, or OD) and one is measured inside the tube wall (the inside diameter, or ID).

You can find tubing in a variety of shapes—round, square, and oval—and in a variety of metals. Slicing tubing to different lengths and profiles is an easy way to create different elements for a modular piece.

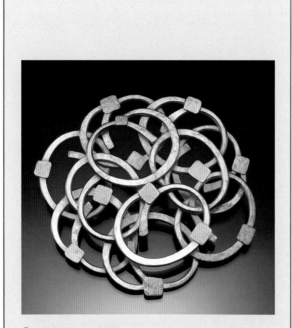

● **LOEBER + LOOK**
Rose Brooch, 2005
5.5 x 6.2 x 0.8 cm
18-karat gold, sterling silver wire; hand cut,
hand forged, soldered
Photo by Ralph Gabriner

● **KRISTIN LORA**
Tubular Rings, 2006
2.5 x 2.5 x 2.5 cm
Sterling silver tubing, stock, and ring
band; hand cut, hand fabricated,
soldered
Photo by Sara Stathas

Blanks and Preformed Metal Sheets

Blanks, sometimes called stampings, are flat pieces of metal available in different sizes and shapes, such as squares, ovals, circles, and rectangles; they are also available in various base and precious metals. You can order them from jewelry suppliers.

Preformed metal sheets, available at some home improvement centers or from industrial suppliers, are flat pieces of metal perforated in a variety of patterns. You can cut out sections of the sheet to create your own particular pattern and design.

Two patterns of preformed metal sheet

Metal blanks in various shapes, sizes, and colors

Sheet Metal

If you need flat metal in a particular size and shape not available in manufactured form, sheet metal is the way to go. You can find flat sheets of both precious and base metals in different sizes and thicknesses. As with metal wires, the thickness of sheet metal is referred to as its gauge. From one manufacturer to the next, the same gauge sheet metal may vary slightly in thickness, but the differences shouldn't be enough to affect the results of your jewelry.

Sheet metal in copper, silver, and gold

● SARAH HOOD
Drop Earrings, 2006
5 x 1.5 x 0.3 cm
Sterling silver discs, cable chain, and earwires; soldered, hand finished
Photo by Doug Yaple

● LOEBER + LOOK
Chex Necklace, 2006
1.5 x 45.5 x 0.3 cm
Sterling silver tubing; hand cut, soldered
Photo by Ralph Gabriner

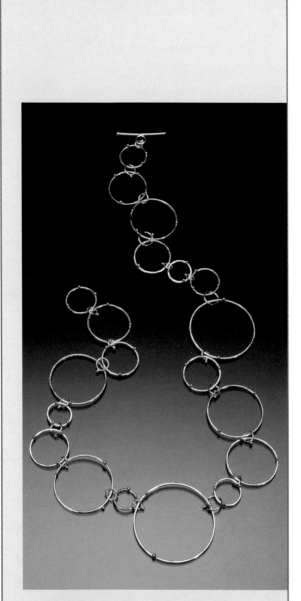

Jewelry Supplies

Besides the flat pieces mentioned above, any good jewelry supply catalog or store can sell a number of other components you can include in your modular pieces. These include bangles, balls, beads, rings, and more.

When designing a piece such as a necklace, one element to consider carefully is the chain that will hold it together. A chain, if you think about it, is inherently modular—it's a series of small, standardized pieces brought together in a single design. Chains are available in a variety of materials, thicknesses, and patterns.

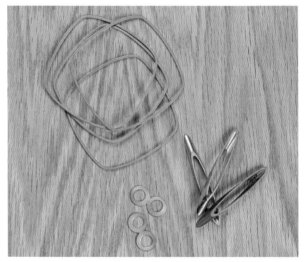

Brass bangles and other jewelry supplies

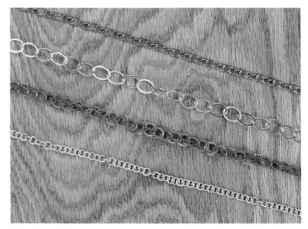

Jewelry chains

Commercial Hardware

The number of types of commercial hardware you can use in a piece may only be limited by the length of the hardware aisle in your local store and the breadth of your imagination. You can use washers, nuts, pins, hooks, chains, and more—all available in several different sizes and often in different metals and finishes.

An assortment of nuts and washers

Jewelry Findings

Findings are premade pieces available from jewelry supply stores and catalogs. Commercial findings come in many different metal types, including gold, gold-filled, sterling silver, brass, surgical steel, and more. Some types of findings can make it easier to assemble a piece of jewelry; these include settings, bezels, bead and end caps, crimp beads, jump rings, and head and eye pins. Other findings are used to make a piece wearable: bales, clasps, pin backs, ear wires, ear posts, nuts, and others.

Left: Clasps for bracelets and necklaces **Right:** Earring findings, from left: ear posts, nuts, French wires, and kidney wires

● **2 ROSES**
OfficeWear Contemporary Necklace, 2007
45 x 45 x 0.6 cm
Steel spring clips; cold connected
Photo by John Lemieux Rose

BASIC TOOLS AND MATERIALS

Whatever kind of jewelry you are making, certain tools and materials are standard for cutting, shaping, preparing, or finishing the elements in your final piece.

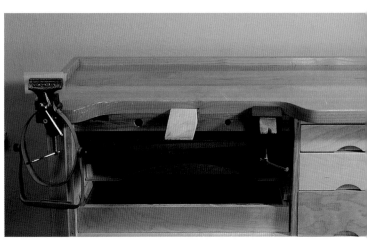

A jeweler's bench

Assorted bench pins and a clamp

Jeweler's Bench and Bench Pin

A jeweler's bench is a wooden workstation specifically designed to meet the needs of metalsmiths. It has such features as tool drawers, catch trays, and precut holes to hold bench pins and mandrels. It is also built at the right height for healthy metalworking. A good-quality jeweler's bench is not inexpensive. However, a sturdy wooden table with an attachable clamp to hold a bench pin is a perfectly acceptable setup if you're just starting out. A standard wooden bench pin is used to support metal for sawing, filing, etc. Most pins have a V-shaped slot cut in at least one side.

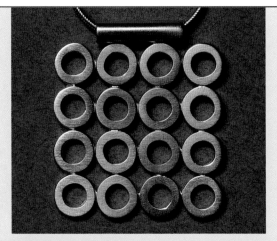

● **KATHLEEN DIRESTA**
Circle Grid Necklace, 2002
3 x 3 x 0.2 cm
Sterling silver, 18-karat gold; handmade, cast
Photo by Storm Photo

● **JENNY WINDLER**
Rattle-Ring, 2004
3.2 x 2.5 x 2.5 cm
Sterling silver, hose filter gasket, steel ball bearings; hand cut, soldered
Photo by Haley Bates

Measuring and Marking Tools

I think it was a carpenter rather than a jewelry maker who came up with the expression "Measure twice, cut once," but it is good advice for any craft, especially one using precious materials. (At the very least, be awfully sure about your first measurement before you get out the cutting tools.) Here are some tools that will make the process of measuring and marking easier and more precise.

Scribe

A scribe is a pointed tool used to make marks on metal. You'll use a scribe to draw points and lines or to transfer designs. You can purchase a commercial scribe, or just make your own scribe by sharpening the end of a piece of scrap metal, such as a nail.

Stainless Steel Ruler

The precision and durability of a short (about 6-inch or 15.2-cm) stainless steel ruler is invaluable to any jeweler. Steel rulers are commonly available in a 12-inch

Marking tools, from left: templates, compass, and center punch

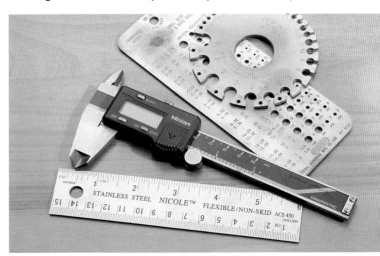

Measuring tools, from top right: wire gauge, drill bit gauge, digital calipers, and steel ruler

● **JENNY WINDLER**
Little Bearing, 2005
2.5 x 1.9 x 1.9 cm
Sterling silver, found ball bearings, brass; hand cut, formed, soldered, cold connected
Photo by artist

● **KATHLEEN DIRESTA**
Mod Circle Bracelet, 2003
1.5 x 15 x 0.2 cm
Sterling silver, 18-karat gold, 14-karat white gold, diamonds; handmade, cast
Photo by Ralph Gabriner

(30.5 cm) size as well, though a shorter ruler is easier to work with for small surfaces and small objects. Choose a steel ruler with lengths given in small, easily divisible metric increments, such as centimeters and millimeters, on one side and with lengths in inches on the other. Most measurements in this book will be given in both inches and in metric figures, except for certain jewelry parts and tools (such as small drill bits) whose measurements are normally given only in metric.

Separators and Calipers

Separators make measuring equal distances simple and precise. Simply set the two metal arms apart at the desired space, lock in this length, and measure the metal.

Calipers are used chiefly to measure thickness (gauge) or diameter. Each pair usually has two adjustable jaws. Use calipers to measure sheet metal, wire, rod, or tubing gauge. Calipers are either digital, with an LCD screen, or analogue, with a dial. Digital calipers are more accurate, but also much more expensive.

Templates

Having a selection of design templates is helpful for scribing common shapes onto metal. The templates can be plastic or metal with various sizes of cutout circles, ovals, squares, triangles, and more. If you need an instrument for measuring angles, a protractor can help you draw and plot your design.

Cutting Tools

Once you've measured and marked precisely, one of the following tools will cut your material to the size and length you need.

Shears, Snips, and Clippers

With handheld metal shears, you can cut straight or curved lines in metal sheet. Shears with smaller blades allow you to

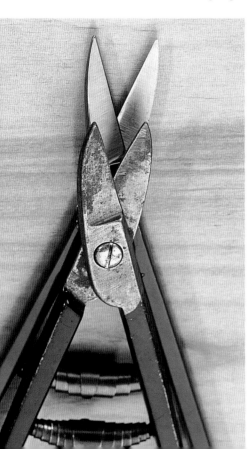

Metal shears

cut more intricate contours and patterns. Larger, table-mounted shears are also available. Snips, also known as cutters, are made for cutting wire. They have either flush or angled blades. Large-size nail clippers are also handy for cutting some types of wire.

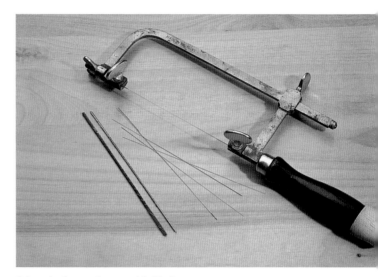

A jeweler's saw frame with blades

Jeweler's Saw Frame and Blades

A high-quality, well-balanced jeweler's saw is one of the most important tools you can buy for working with metal. The open frame is made of rigid steel and can be adjusted for blade length and tension. The saw grip should be comfortable to hold. The throat depth of a jeweler's saw is the distance from the blade to the opposite vertical frame element. On standard frames, the throat depth ranges from 2¼ to 6 inches (5.7 to 15.2 cm). There are also jeweler's saws made with very deep frames for working on oversized projects. The throat depth of these frames is about 11 inches (27.9 cm). Jeweler's saw blades must be periodically replaced as they become dull or break. The saw frame is engineered to make this switch as easy as possible, using setscrews or clamps to hold the blade in place.

Saw blades are made from steel and steel alloys. They are manufactured in different sizes, with 1/0, 2/0, and 3/0 being the most popular; other sizes up to 8/0 are also available. As with the gauge system, the numbers here work inversely: a 3/0 blade is thicker and wider (and relatively more "coarse") than a 6/0 blade (relatively more "fine").

Each commercial brand of blade has a slightly different thickness, depth, and number of teeth per 1 inch (2.5 cm). Most jewelry-making supply catalogues provide this information, along with the correct size blade for each metal gauge and the drill size required for using a blade when piercing and cutting metal. Good saw blades have straight, uniform teeth and are flexible. Better-quality saw blades are more expensive, of course, but they resist breakage and last longer, usually until they become dull. Less expensive blades are more likely to snap or break, especially when used by beginners. The more sawing experience you gain, the longer your blades will last.

A handheld tube-cutting jig with tubing

Tube-cutting Jig

Many of the jewelry pieces in this book take advantage of the wide variety of metal tubes and rods that are commercially available. Using a tube-cutting jig with your jeweler's saw makes it easier to get neat, straight cuts through tubes and rods every time. This helpful tool has a stop you can set to cut pieces to a particular length—this is a very big help when you need 24 slices of tubing all exactly 5 mm long.

PEGGY R. COCHRAN
Bent, Pendant, 2005
5.1 x 1.3 x 1.3 cm
Sterling silver snake chain tubing and wire, copper; hand cut, solder fabricated
Photo by Courtney Frisse

An assortment of hand files

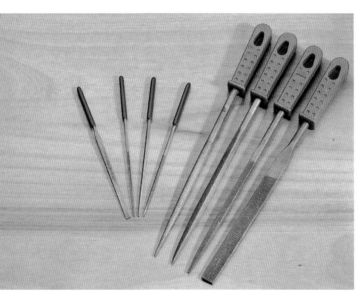

An assortment of needle files

Sandpapers, sanding sticks, sanding pads, and steel wool

Smoothing Tools

After a piece is cut, you'll need to smooth all sharp edges. Smoothing tools can also be used to alter the shape and texture of pieces.

Files

Metal files are constructed from a strong, tool-steel alloy and, with proper care, they should last a long time. Manual files used to remove, shape, or finish metal are called (naturally) hand files. These are generally 8 inches (20.3 cm) in total length with a cutting distance of 6 inches (15.2 cm). A hand file's "cut" size can range from very coarse to very fine. For removing metal quickly, start with the coarsest file, then switch to medium "cuts," and finally the finest file. Hand files also come with many different profiles; the most popular are flat, barrette, half round, and square. Many more contours are offered so you can more closely match the shape of the file to the shape of your metalwork.

Needle files are shorter, usually only 6 inches (15.2 cm) in total length, and much more narrow than hand files. Needle files have a fine cut that is perfect for finishing and smoothing small metal elements, and their thin shape makes it easy to reach into tight areas. They are also available in different cut sizes and contours. Some needle files have diamond particles attached, and these can be used to shape ceramic and glass as well as metal.

Sanding Papers, Pads, and Sticks

Abrasive papers used to sand metal are made differently from those for sanding wood. Their grit is attached to the paper with a stronger fixative. This bond allows the abrasive to effectively shape and finish the metal, and it gives the paper a longer working life and the ability to be used both wet and dry. Metal sanding papers come in many grit sizes from coarse to fine. Higher-numbered papers have finer grits. Most jewelers prefer 220-, 400-, and 600-grit papers. When you are finishing a piece, you commonly begin with a coarser, higher-numbered grit, and then gradually work with finer and finer grits until a sufficiently smooth finish is achieved. Green kitchen scrub pads and different grades of steel wool are also often used for sanding and finishing metal.

Varieties of hammers, from left: chasing, ball-peen, forging, goldsmith's, small ball-peen, and riveting

Hammering Tools

Hammers and mallets are useful for flattening, forming, or shaping metal.

Chasing Hammer

Specifically designed and weighted for metalworking, the head of a chasing hammer is made of polished steel and has two faces with different shapes. One face is wide, smooth, and slightly convex. Use it for striking other tools or for planishing (flattening) metal. The opposite end is ball-shaped. Use it for riveting and peening.

Mallets

Wooden, rawhide, or rubber mallets are very helpful tools for forming, bending, and flattening metal. With wide cylindrical heads and two flat faces, they move metal without marring, scratching, or damaging its surface. Although less common, plastic and nylon mallets can perform the same functions as wooden or rawhide ones.

Steel Block

Whether you're working at a jeweler's bench or on a worktable, it's most effective to hammer and form metal on top of a rigid steel block. The best bench blocks are made from tool steel that has been ground flat and polished. You can purchase one from a jewelry supply store or make your own. Most blocks range from 2½ to 5 inches (6.4 to 12.7 cm) square.

● **JAMES THURMAN**
Quarter Bracelet, 1994
5 x 5.7 x 2.5 cm
Silver coins, sterling silver sheet; hand cut, formed, soldered
Photo by artist

● **SIM LUTTIN**
Just Dandy, 2007
Diameter, 7 cm
Sterling silver wire; cold connected
Photo by Kevin Montague

Forming Tools

When you are hammering metal, it is often to change its shape. These tools can provide a shape to form a piece around, or help to flatten and shape a material in particular ways.

Metal and wooden mandrels

A mallet, steel block, daps, and dapping block

Dapping Blocks and Daps

A dapping block contains a number of concave domes in different sizes. Placing a piece of sheet metal or other jewelry component over a particular hole and then striking it with a round-ended metal or wooden dap and a mallet can create a variety of dome shapes and curved profiles.

Mandrels

A mandrel is any type of sturdy form around which you can shape, straighten, or size metal. Commercial ring, bracelet, and necklace mandrels are made of metal or wood. Ring mandrels are tapered and marked with standard ring sizes. Bracelet mandrels have a gradual taper without markings, and necklace mandrels are designed to show how a piece will drape on the neck. You can hammer metal directly on or around most commercial mandrels. Feel free to use any common household item as a mandrel. Dowels and rods—or even pencils, knitting needles, chopsticks, and rolling pins—can all do the job of a mandrel in particular situations.

Rolling Mill

This useful metalworking machine has two round rollers with an adjustable space between them. Turning the long handle feeds a flat material, usually sheet metal, between the rollers. Depending on the rollers and the settings used, you can make the metal thinner, imprint a design on it, or do special tasks such as creating round or square metal wire.

A rolling mill

Pliers, clockwise from left: round-nose pliers, snips, needle-nose pliers, and flat-nose pliers

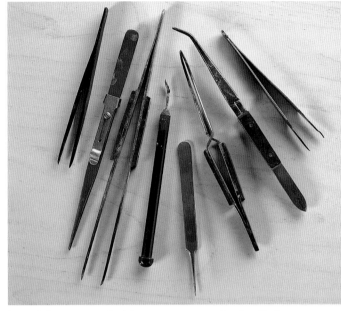

From left: tweezers, locking tweezers, wooden-handled tweezers, solder pick, micro-nose tweezers, straight cross-locking tweezers, bent cross-locking tweezers, and tweezers

Holding Tools

The following tools are used to hold, bend, or twist materials. You can use them to open up the closed ends of a jump ring, safely hold a tiny component to the end of a torch's flame, or help with many other tasks.

Pliers

Jeweler's pliers come in many different forms, most of them easily identifiable by a name that corresponds to their jaw shape. **Round-nose pliers** have fully rounded jaws that taper up from the base. Use them for looping wire, making jump rings, and bending wire and sheet. **Chain-nose pliers** are round on the outside of the jaw but flat on the inside, tapering up to a point. Use them for bending wire and sheet. **Flat-nose pliers** have flat and flush interior surfaces. The outside surfaces of their jaws are flat and angled. Use them to grip metal as you work and to create angular bends. Round-nose, chain-nose, and flat-nose pliers are commonly made of stainless steel or tool steel and are available in short and long jaw lengths. You can also find many other specialty pliers to make particular tasks easier.

Tweezers and Third Hands

Tweezers are helpful for holding very small objects, and for safely working with high heat in processes such as soldering and annealing. Locking tweezers make it easier to hold onto materials when you are doing several things at once.

Another helpful tool is a variation on locking tweezers known as a "third hand." This tool commonly has a base that sits on your table or workbench, and it contains a set of locking jaws (similar to a pair of tweezers or small pliers) that can firmly hold a piece in place above the work surface. These are available with a single set of jaws, and also with two sets of jaws to hold two pieces at once. (Maybe that type should be called a "third and fourth hand.")

Drilling Tools

To pierce, rivet, or string jewelry components, you may have to create a hole or holes through them. Drilling pieces as small as those you encounter in jewelry making can be daunting at first, but it becomes easier with a little practice.

From bottom: center punch and automatic center punch

Center Punch

A center punch is a tool with one pointed end used to make a small dent on a metal surface prior to drilling. Standard center punches have one flat end that must be tapped with a hammer to make an indention. Automatic punches have an adjustable internal hammer that releases when the punch is pressed down on the metal. You can use a nail as a center punch if you sharpen its tip.

Flexible Shaft Machine

A flexible shaft machine, or flex shaft, is the jeweler's equivalent of a drill, but you can use it for much more than just drilling holes (though it works wonderfully for that). It consists of a motor and a hand piece to which many devices, such as drill bits, burrs, cutters, and sanding disks, can be attached. Most flexible shaft machines are run by foot pedals, allowing you to control the speed of the motor. A long, flexible shaft connects the motor to the hand piece. It is important to keep a wide arch in the shaft so the machine will run safely and efficiently. A narrow arch or crimp near the motor or hand piece can cause premature wear and excess heat. For this reason, it's a good idea to mount the motor of the flex shaft on a stand above your worktable or bench.

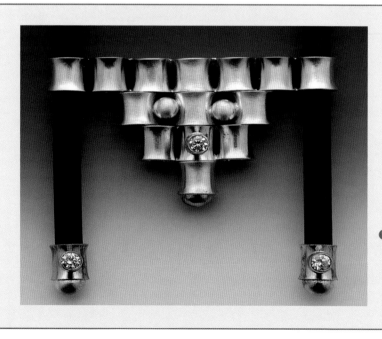

● **CHRISTINE DHEIN**
Flare Necklace, 2002
30 x 15 x 0.7 cm
18-karat gold, sterling silver, rubber, diamonds; hand fabricated, tube set
Photo by George Post

A flexible shaft machine with accessories

Jeweler's drill bits (left) and diamond drill bits (right)

Drill Bits

Metal drill bits for jewelry making are much smaller than average drill bits. The chuck in the flexible shaft machine is specially sized to accommodate these smaller attachments. Most bits are made from hard and polished steel and can sustain the high speeds of the flex shaft. Most bits are measured by their diameter in millimeters, but some are manufactured and labeled to correspond with wire gauge sizes.

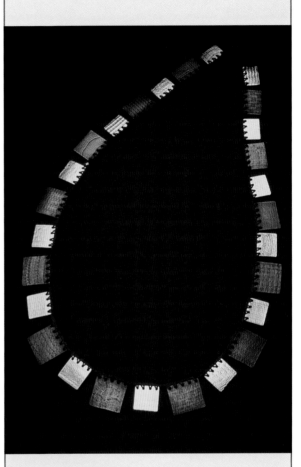

ERICA SCHLUETER
Tab Necklace, 2007
Sterling silver sheet, 18-karat gold and silver bi-metal sheet, silk, patina; roller printed, hand cut, crocheted
Photo by Bill Lemke

Finishing Tools and Materials

Some of the tools discussed in the previous section on smoothing tools—such as sandpapers and steel wool—are also important parts of your arsenal for giving an attractive, durable finish to a piece. Other tools and materials you may use for this purpose include the following.

A tumbler and steel shot with (from left) steel brush, flexible shaft attachments, steel wool, and polishing cloth

Coloring agents, from left: liver of sulfur, selenium toner, and black patina solution

Patinas and Colorings

The color and texture of the materials you use in making jewelry need only be a starting point. The surface of metal can take on many different appearances.

Applying a patina is a simple process that adds depth and color to metal, especially if its surface is textured or has a design. Three solutions you can use to create a colored finish on metal are **liver of sulfur, selenium toner,** and **black patina.** You can purchase liver of sulfur and black patinas from jewelry suppliers, and you can find selenium toner at photography stores. An important safety note: Always read and follow the manufacturer's instructions when working with chemical patinas.

A polishing machine

Tumblers and Polishing Machines

Heavy-grit **steel wool** or a **brass brush** can create a shinier finish. Another way to work the finish of metal is to put it in a **tumbler** with pieces of shot (commonly stainless steel) and usually water and a little soap. This process will help to shine and burnish the metal.

A **polishing machine,** which spins buffing wheels to hold the piece against, can be used with various polishing compounds to produce an extremely shiny finish. You can also use smaller polishing wheels and attachments in your flexible shaft; this may work better for smaller pieces.

● **LESLIE C. GORDON**
Untitled, 2005
Bracelet: 20 x 1 cm; Earrings: 3.5 x 1 cm;
Ring: 2 x 2 x 1 cm
Sterling silver tubing; fabricated, soldered, sliced
Photo by Pier L. DelFrate, The Foto Shop

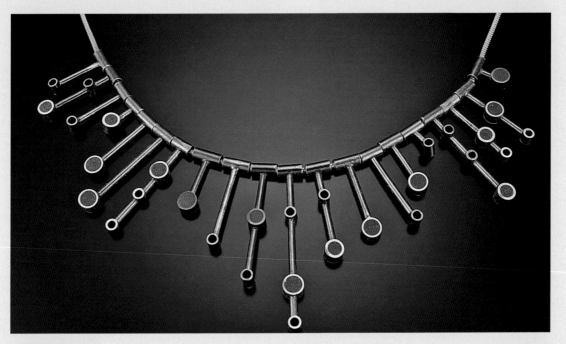

● **SADIE WANG**
Red Resin Circle Dangle Necklace, 2006
4.5 x 40.6 x 0.3 cm
Sterling silver, resin; hand fabricated
Photo by Azad Photo

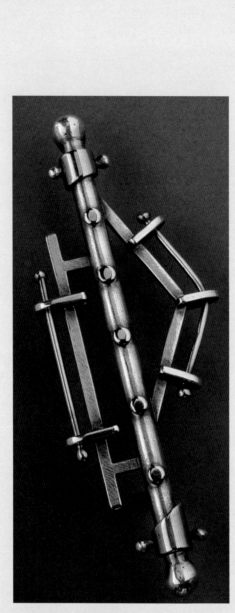

● **PEGGY R. COCHRAN**
Figurative Study #2, Brooch, 2004
7.6 x 3.8 x 1.9 cm
**Sterling silver, brass, 14-karat gold
wire; solder fabricated
Photo by Courtney Frisse**

ASSEMBLY TOOLS AND MATERIALS

Once you've taken your basic materials and then cut, filed, and shaped them, you've got to put them together. That's where the following tools and materials come in.

Cold Connection Tools and Materials

Components frequently are put together into jewelry with cold connections. Three common ways to join or attach components are with settings, rivets, and adhesives.

An assortment of jump rings

Jump Rings

Wire circles, known as jump rings, are one of the simplest ways to hold jewelry components together. The rings are split so they can be opened and closed with pliers. You can buy these commercially or make your own; you'll find out how to do that in the section that follows on Skills and Techniques.

Some tips for using jump rings: To open and close a jump ring, move its ends so they no longer meet, but without pulling them apart and distorting the ring's round shape. Two pairs of needle-nose pliers work well for this. Also, to maintain a jump ring's shape and strength, only open it as far as needed to insert the objects being joined.

Rivets

One strong and secure way to attach two pieces of metal together is through rivets. We'll discuss them in more detail in the section on Skills and Techniques.

One tool to have on hand for making rivets is a **flaring tool.** It stretches open, or flares, the ends of tube rivets. These metal tools are available commercially or can be homemade from any number of materials as long as one end is tapered and one is flat for hammering. A worn-out flexible shaft attachment or an old chasing tool makes a fine flaring tool.

Burnishers

A burnisher is a versatile metalworking hand tool. Use it to gently shape and smooth metals, to open or close bezel settings, to even out surface imperfections, and to polish hard-to-reach places. Standard burnishers have wooden handles for a comfortable grip. The working end of the tool may be straight or bent.

If you want to use an adhesive to join jewelry components, choose one that bonds quickly and stays strong. A colorless adhesive is generally preferable. Two-part epoxy comes in two vials or syringes, the contents of which combine to form a very strong

Metalworking tools, from bottom: burnishers, bezel pusher, and prong pusher

bond. Besides working well with metal, epoxies can bond strongly with a wide variety of materials including plastic, rubber, leather, stone, glass, and ceramics. Follow the manufacturer's directions to mix the specific proportions of the two parts together, stirring it with a wooden tongue depressor (or, for a small amount, a toothpick), and applying it quickly. Use epoxies in a well-ventilated area, and avoid breathing the fumes. Cyanoacrylate glues bond similar and dissimilar materials instantly—including your skin—so use them with care.

Wire Wrapping

Wire is a simple connector to use in cold connected jewelry. You can bend, wrap, sew, crochet, knit, twist, loop, and coil wire around components. Wire wrapping requires very few tools. All you need is an assortment of pliers and wire cutters or a jeweler's saw.

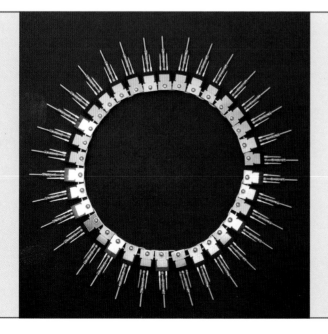

● **2 ROSES**
Hi-Tek Byzantium, 2006
45 x 45 x 0.6 cm
Electrical resistors, electrical connectors, 24-karat gold, sterling silver; hand fabricated
Photo by Corliss Rose

Soldering Tools and Materials

Soldering is another technique you can use to construct and connect jewelry components. It requires using a torch and solder to heat and bind metal. The following are some of the tools and materials you need for this technique.

Firebrick

Soldering must be done on top of a surface that is heat-resistant. One way to create this surface is with a layer of firebrick. These are the same bricks used inside ceramic kilns, and they can be purchased from any home improvement center.

A soldering torch with oxy-acetylene tanks

A soldering station with (from left) pickle pot, copper tongs, tripod, firebrick, third arm, flux, torch, striker, and solder pick

Soldering Torch and Tanks

To solder you must have heat, and this heat is most often produced by a flame. This flame comes from a torch where a gas and either air or oxygen combine and are lit. The most easily accessible and reasonably priced gas to use for soldering is propane, although acetylene, which burns hotter than propane, is also very popular. Two separate tanks, one for the gas and one for the air or oxygen, are required. Each is fitted with a regulator used to set and maintain pressure and gas flow. Individual hoses, color-coded for safety, are attached to the regulators and run to the torch handle. A tip is attached to the handle to shape the size of the flame.

Soldering Flux

Solder flows only on a clean metal surface. If oxygen reaches the surface of the metal when it is heated, oxides form. Flux is a substance that promotes the fusion of metals by forming a layer that blocks the oxygen. Before soldering, use a

Flux materials, from left: flux brush, flux container with small tip, spray bottle, paste flux, and liquid flux

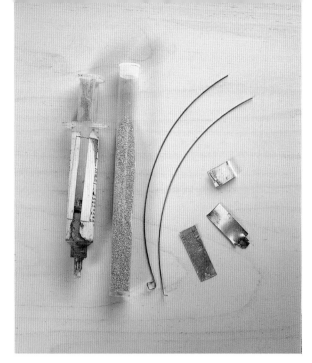

Solder varieties, from left: paste solder, powdered solder, wire solder, and sheet solder

paintbrush to apply flux to the surfaces to be joined to facilitate their union. Different types of flux are effective at different heat levels, most commonly between 1100° and 1500°F (593° and 815°C). Be sure to use the flux that corresponds to your soldering temperature. You'll find charts for the melting temperatures of different metals and for solder flow points on page 123.

Solder

Solder is a metal alloy that, when melted, joins metallic surfaces. Different types of metal and different process-es require the use of different solders. Gold and silver solders, alloyed to a lower melting temperature than the metals they join, are the most common. Within these two main categories there are several varieties of solder based on the temperature at which they melt, also known as the flow point. For silver solders, the most common are **easy** (also called **soft**), **medium,** and **hard** (listed in order of increasing flow point). Gold solders are identified by their karat (generally 10, 14, or 16). Lower karat gold solders have lower melting temperatures than higher karat gold solders. The flow points for silver solders are standardized (see the chart on page 123), but the flow points of gold solders may

vary from manufacturer to manufacturer, so ask your supplier for a data sheet.

Solder is sold in several forms, the most popular being **wire** and **sheet.** You can also purchase **paste solder,** which is a mixture of tiny bits of solder with a paste flux. Choose the type you like best for the soldering method needed.

Pickle

Pickle is an acidic compound that removes flux and oxi-dized surfaces from soldered metal. Many varieties can be used, the most common being sodium bisulphate, which is also used to clean swimming pools. This chemical is available from jewelry suppliers. Nontoxic substitutes include alum or a solution of vinegar and salt. To obtain the fast-est results, use pickle that's been heated in a slow cooker dedicated to this process.

SKILLS AND TECHNIQUES

Some basic skills, such as sawing, are essential for most metalworking. Other skills are useful depending on the type of jewelry you'd like to make and the equipment you have. Read through the different procedures carefully, then give them a trial run.

Sawing Metal

To saw metal, you'll need a jeweler's saw and saw blades, a bench pin, and sheet metal. If you're new to this, it's a good idea to first practice on a scrap sheet, rather than an essential component.

Installing a Saw Blade into a Saw Frame

1. Open the saw frame's jaw approximately ³/₈ inch (9.5 mm) shorter than the length of the blade. Insert the blade into the top nut of the frame, with the teeth facing away from the neck and pointing down. Tighten the nut.

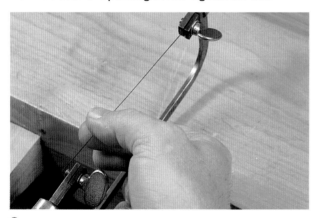

2. Rest the end of the saw frame handle on your sternum, and rest the top edge of the saw frame against the edge of a worktable or jeweler's bench. Use your sternum to press the saw handle and slightly shorten the length of the jaw.

3. Place the free end of the saw blade into the lower nut, and tighten. Release the pressure on the saw handle. The blade should be stretched tight in the frame.

Sawing Steps

1. Hold the saw lightly in your hand. Only use your hand to guide the saw, and do not exert pressure against the metal. The temptation to press too hard is great, and most beginning metalworkers break a lot of saw blades that way. Don't worry if this happens to you. Success and ease comes through practice.

2. Place the metal on the bench pin. Position the saw blade at a 90° angle to the metal. Move the saw frame up and down, keeping the frame pointing forward. The teeth of the blade will cut the metal only on the downward stroke.

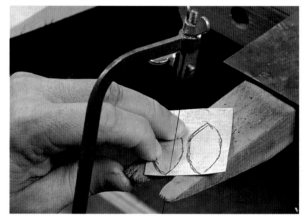

3. Turn the metal, not the saw frame, when making a rounded cut. To make a tight rounded cut, simultaneously turn the metal and the saw while quickly moving the frame up and down.

Filing Metal

All sawed metal pieces have sharp edges that should be removed with a file for safe handling. Metal can also be shaped and contoured with a file.

1. Secure the metal to be filed against a worktable or bench. Select the coarsest file needed to begin taking away the metal.

2. Place your index finger on the top of the file. Press down as you slide the file forward against the metal. Lift the file off the metal as you bring it back and reposition it for another stroke.

Note: The teeth on the file are angled away from the handle. This means that all cutting is accomplished on the file's forward stroke. Applying pressure on the back stroke will only wear down the file.

3. If necessary, repeat steps 1 and 2 with a sequence of finer files to make the edges the required shape and smoothness.

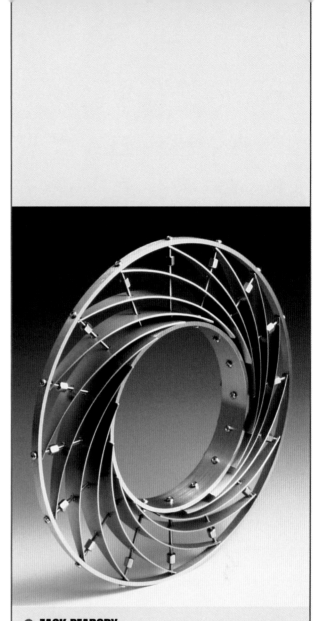

● **ZACK PEABODY**
Turbine Bracelet, 1997
13 x 13 x 2 cm
Stainless steel, titanium;
cold connected
Photo by artist

Filing metal with a file and bench pin

Making Jump Rings

As I mentioned in the section on Assembly Tools and Materials, you can buy a variety of commercially manufactured jump rings. But making your own jump rings is easy, will save you money, and gives you control over the exact size and material of the jump rings you use in your projects. Here's how to do it.

MATERIALS

* Wire, gauge and metal of your choice

TOOLS AND SUPPLIES

* Mandrel, diameter equal to the inside dimension of the jump rings you want to make
* Wire snips
* Jeweler's saw and blades

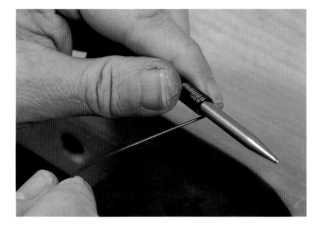

1. Cut a piece of wire and wrap it tightly around the mandrel, making sure that each of the coils (which will each make one jump ring) is touching against the coil below it. Snip the wire when the coil is about 1 to 1½ inches long (2.5 to 3.8 cm).

2. Hold the coil in your fingers on top of your bench pin or working surface. With your other hand holding the saw against the top coil at a slight angle, begin to carefully saw down the length of the coil.

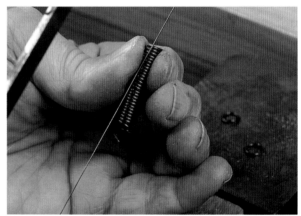

● SARAH HOOD
Disc Bracelet, 2006
1 x 18.5 x 0.3 cm
Sterling silver discs and cable chain; soldered, hand finished
Photo by Doug Yaple

Forming and Annealing Metal

For most of the projects in this book, forming and annealing your material won't be necessary. That's one of the advantages of starting with preformed, manufactured materials. I mentioned earlier that in some cases you may decide to use sheet metal when manufactured materials are not available in the size and shape you want. In those cases, annealing metal (a process that makes it more workable) may be necessary.

Here's why: To form sheet metal is to coax it into a dimensional shape. There are many techniques you can use to accomplish this. Bending by hand is perhaps the most simple. Other options include hammering sheet around a mandrel or into a depression, using a dapping block and dap, forging, and using a die press. When metal is formed, especially with a hammer, its molecular structure changes. The longer it's worked, the harder and more brittle it becomes. This change

is called work hardening, and it can be reversed through the process of annealing.

Annealing loosens the molecular structure of hardened metal to make it malleable once again. Different metals are annealed in different ways, but they are all based on heat. To anneal silver and gold alloys, paint a paste flux onto the metal, place it on a fire-resistant surface, and heat it to approximately 1100°F (593°C) (see photo A). At the correct annealing temperature, the flux liquefies and turns clear—a good visual indicator. (You can find a chart on annealing temperatures for different metals on page 123.) Allow the piece to slightly cool until any reddish hue disappears, then use tongs to quench the annealed metal in water (photo B). When annealing copper, heat the metal until it glows dull red before quenching. Brass should be heated until it is clearly red-hot, allowed to cool for a minute, then quenched.

● **SIM LUTTIN**
Distorted Horizon #3, 2006
6 x 1.5 cm
Fine silver, nylon and steel cord,
magnets; roller printed,
hand fabricated, soldered
Photos by Kevin Montague

Riveting

A rivet is a piece of wire or tube fed through a hole and flared on each end to hold two pieces of metal together. Rivets are very practical, attractive ways to cold connect jewelry parts. The following instructions show you how to make a wire or tube rivet.

MATERIALS

- Sheet metal to be joined
- Wire or tubing for rivet

TOOLS AND SUPPLIES

- Calipers (preferred) or metal ruler
- Jeweler's saw and saw blades
- Wet/dry sandpaper
- Drill bit, same diameter as wire or tube rivet
- Steel block
- Center punch
- Chasing hammer
- Flexible shaft machine or small motorized rotary tool
- Flaring tool (for tube rivets only)

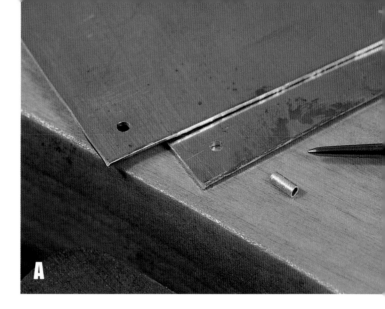

A

1. Use calipers or a ruler to measure the combined thickness of the metals to be joined. Add approximately 2 mm to this measurement.

2. Use the jeweler's saw to cut a corresponding length of wire or tube. Sand the ends of the cut wire or tube.

3. Using a bit that is the same diameter as the wire or tube, drill a hole through each metal piece at the point they are to be riveted (as in photo A). Thread the wire or tube through the drilled holes, and place the metal on top of a steel block.

● **SARAH HOOD**
Carnelian Lotus Bracelet, 2006
2.5 x 18.5 x 0.5 cm
Sterling silver discs and cable chain, coin-cut carnelian; engraved, soldered, hand finished
Photos by Doug Yaple

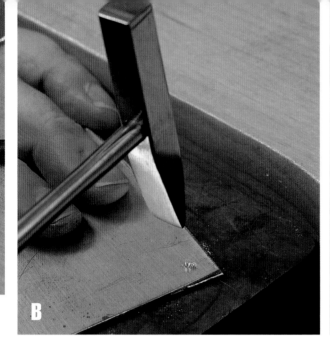

For wire riveting: gently tap one end of the wire two or three times with a chasing hammer (see photo B). Turn over the metal piece and adjust the wire so there is an equal length sticking out of each side of the hole. Gently tap two or three times on the reverse side. Repeat this process—tapping, turning, and adjusting-until the wire ends flare, forming the rivet and making a secure connection.

For tube riveting: insert a flaring tool into one end of the tubing. Use a chasing hammer to make one light tap on the flaring tool (see photo C). Turn over the metal piece, insert the flaring tool into the opposite tubing end, and make another light tap. Repeat this process, adjusting the tube so an equal length sticks out of each side of the hole, and make one tap on each tubing end until the tubing cannot be removed from the hole. At this point, tap gently and directly on the tubing with the ball side of the chasing hammer. Repeatedly turn the metal over in order to tap an equal amount on both sides until the rivet is secure.

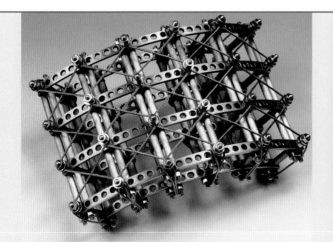

● **ZACK PEABODY**
Brooch 534, 1992
7 x 5 x 3 cm
Stainless steel, niobium; cold connected
Photos by artist

Soldering

Hot metalworking often involves soldering. This process permanently joins two pieces of metal together with heat, flux, and solder. Practicing this technique is the best way to learn and perfect the process. Follow these steps to ensure a strong and good-looking solder joint. (The how-to photographs shown here illustrate pick soldering.)

Soldering Set

There are specific tools and materials you'll use every time you solder. For a number of the projects in this book, you'll see a reference in the Tools list to a "Soldering set" that will refer you back to this page. To solder elements in those projects, have the following tools and materials on hand. Be sure to read project directions carefully to learn the right type of solder and the specific soldering tools you'll need.

MATERIALS

- Metal components to be joined
- Soldering flux
- Solder (hard, medium, and easy [sometimes called "soft"])

TOOLS AND SUPPLIES

- Safety glasses
- Scrub pad or abrasive paper
- Heat-resistant surface, such as a soldering brick
- Third-arm tweezers
- Small paintbrush for applying soldering flux
- Propane or acetylene soldering torch
- Sharp tweezers
- Copper tongs
- Warmed pickle in a pot, such as a slow cooker

● **KRISTIN LORA**
Square Felt Ball Bracelet, 2006
17.8 x 2.5 x 2.5 cm
Sterling silver tubing and jump rings, felt balls; cast, soldered, cold connected
Photo by Sara Stathas

1. Use a scrub pad or abrasive paper to clean the two metal elements to be soldered. Place them on top of a heat-resistant surface. Position the metal so the seam to be joined is flush. Use a paintbrush to apply flux to the seam (photo A).

2. Use the flux-coated brush to pick up the small solder pieces, called pallions, and apply them across the fluxed metal seam. Alternately, heat the pallions on top of the firebrick with the torch until they ball up, and place them on the seam with a pick (photo B).

3. Wearing safety glasses, light the torch, adjust the air to make a soft flame, and gently heat the area around the joint. The flux will bubble as the temperature rises (photo C). Use tweezers or a pick to reposition any solder that moves off the seam or to add more solder.

4. Continue heating the piece until the solder flows bright and shiny around the joint (photo D). Turn off the torch. Use copper tongs to quench the soldered metal in a pickle bath. Remove the metal from the acid, rinse it in cold water, and dry it.

Different soldering operations may require the use of different soldering techniques. You may find it easier to use a length of wire solder when connecting a large joint that requires a lot of solder. The wire is placed on the joint once the metal is properly heated, making it less likely than pallions or balls to move out of position. Sweat soldering will be beneficial when you need to permanently attach a smaller metal piece on top of a larger one or to attach findings.

Here are some tips to keep in mind when using solder:

- Solder will work only if the metal joint is fully flush and properly aligned. It will never fill in a gap in a seam.
- Solder will only flow on clean metal.
- The metal must be heated sufficiently for solder to flow.
- Heat flows toward cooler metal. Counter this by directing the torch flame around the seam first, not directly at the joint.
- Solder always flows toward the heat. If metal is unevenly heated, the solder will not stay in the correct position.
- Both solder and flux are only effective within a very specific temperature range. Do not overheat the metal.
- Solder in dim light, if possible, so you can see and react to the color changes of heated metal.
- Use third-arm tweezers to balance awkwardly shaped metal pieces so they sit properly and remain stable during soldering.
- When soldering multiple seams, join the first seam with a hard solder (high melting point), and decrease the solder strength as more seams are added. By doing this, the first seams remain intact when the piece is reheated.
- Store solders by type (easy, medium, and hard) and away from dirt and grease.

THE PROJECTS

In the first part of this book, we covered many of the components that can go into a piece of modular jewelry. Another component you'll find in every successful piece of jewelry is the most important one—a smart and attractive design.

Some projects in the following section put everyday materials to imaginative uses, like the steel washers and shimmering spray paint in Joanna Gollberg's Cerulean Necklace, or the copper plumbing connector in Christine Dhein's Bubbles Ring. Other pieces, like Amy Tavern's Geometry Necklace and Earrings, combine jewelry components you can order from a catalog into a clever design. A number of projects allow you to

make your own creative choices. With Kristin Lora's Galaxy Necklace and Satellite Bracelet set, for example, you're presented with a palette of shapes and techniques you can use to decorate nine squares each on the necklace and bracelet. The specific designs and arrangements are all up to you.

The projects are generally arranged from the easiest to the slightly more difficult ones. If you need at any time to return to the Basics section to brush up on a particular technique, go ahead. As you get more familiar with the methods used for modular pieces, you'll find that making jewelry this way is both fast and fun.

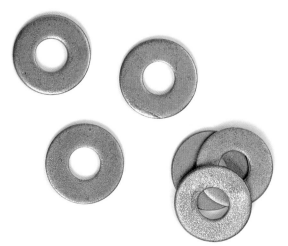

CONNECTION NECKLACE

Using ready-made circles, jump rings, wire, and chain gives you a good head start on making this piece. What brings it to a great finish is how you hammer the wire to subtly shape it, and especially the way that combinations of round and straight, and large and small, fall at different angles as the piece is worn.

Tools

- **Wire cutters**
- **Chasing hammer**
- **Steel block**
- **Fine-tip permanent marking pen**
- **Center punch**
- **Drill bit, #61 size**
- **Flexible shaft**
- **Wooden block for drilling**
- **Sandpaper, 400-grit**
- **2 pairs of flat- or needle-nose pliers**

Parts

- **23 inches (58.4 cm) of 16-gauge sterling silver round wire**
- **14 jump rings, 20-gauge and 5 mm diameter**
- **4 ready-made sterling silver circles: ½, ¾, 1, and 1½ inches (13, 19, 25, and 38 mm) in diameter**
- **16 inches (40.6 cm) of 1.1 mm gauge sterling silver cable chain**
- **2 spring ring clasps, 5 mm diameter**

Assembly

1. With wire cutters, cut ten 2¼-inch (5.7 cm) pieces of the 16-gauge round wire.

2. Using the flat end of a chasing hammer and a steel block, hammer each piece of wire, starting at the center and working toward one end. Hammer with more force as you approach the end. Start at the middle again and hammer in the same way to the other end. The result should be a flattened wire that is wider at the ends.

3. With the marking pen, place a small dot on either end of each piece of wire just a few millimeters from each edge.

4. Use the center punch and chasing hammer on top of the steel block to gently tap a small impression on each dot.

5. Placing the wires on a scrap wooden block, use a #61 drill bit in a flexible shaft to drill holes through the two impressions in each piece.

6. Gently sand away any burs left behind from drilling.

7. To link the components, begin by using two pairs of pliers to open each jump ring. Thread two components through each jump ring in this pattern: three long wire pieces, a 1½-inch (3.8 cm) circle, two long pieces, a 1-inch (2.5 cm) circle, three long pieces, a ¾-inch (1.9 cm) circle, two long pieces, and a ½-inch (1.3 cm) circle. Close rings as you add components. To complete the circle, use a jump ring to connect the first long piece in the pattern with the ½-inch (1.3 cm) circle.

8. Using pliers, hook a spring ring clasp to each end of the cable chain.

9. To complete the assembly, hook one end of the chain to the 1-inch (2.5 cm) circle and the other clasp to the ½-inch (1.3 cm) circle.

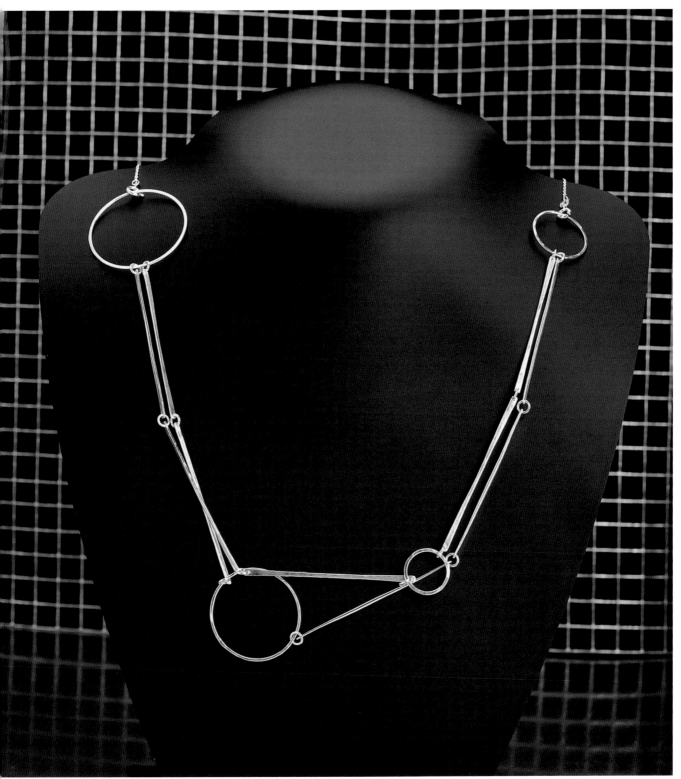

TRANSOM BROOCH

The pattern of the perforated metal sheet in this project—just one of a number of those commercially available—is referred to as Union Jack. Cutting patterned materials like this one and combining them with other shapes gives the piece a strong geometric presence.

Tools

- **Metal shears**
- **Jeweler's saw and blades**
- **Metal file**
- **Two-part epoxy**
- **Drill and small drill bit**

Parts

- **Perforated aluminum sheet, 20-gauge**
- **2 precut acrylic shapes, 1 inch square (2.5 cm)**
- **4-inch-square colored acrylic sheet**
- **2 tie tack pins and clutches**

Assembly

1. Cut out a square of the perforated sheet. In the example shown, the precut shapes dictated the dimensions to which the sheet was cut. The small black square shape was centered on the sheet to accent the diagonal lines of the Union Jack pattern.

2. After cutting the perforated sheet, use a file to clean the metal edges. Take care to file the edges to prevent the metal from catching threads in your clothing.

3. Mark the colored acrylic sheet to the same dimensions of your cut piece of perforated metal sheet. Use a jeweler's saw to carefully cut out the shape, taking care to keep the edges true. File the edges of the cut acrylic shape smooth.

4. Mix a small amount of two-part epoxy according to the manufacturer's instructions. Adhere one of the small precut shapes in the center of one side of the aluminum sheet. Allow the epoxy to cure. Then mix another small amount of epoxy, and adhere the second shape on the opposite side of the metal sheet. Allow the epoxy to cure.

5. Select a drill bit that is approximate in size to the pad on your tie tack pin. Mark and drill two shallow holes spaced approximately 1 inch (2.5 cm) apart in the backside of the cut acrylic shape. Drill the holes just deep enough so that you will be able to slip in the tie tack pads.

6. Mix a small amount of two-part epoxy, spread it in the drilled holes, and place the tie tack pins in the epoxy. Allow the epoxy to cure.

7. Mix another small amount of the epoxy. Apply it to one of the precut shapes; this is the shape that will not face outward and will be mostly hidden. Attach the assembly to the cut acrylic shape. Allow the epoxy to cure.

A side view reveals how this piece sandwiches together a small acrylic square, perforated metal sheet, another small square, and a larger acrylic square. Two tie tack pins make it wearable.

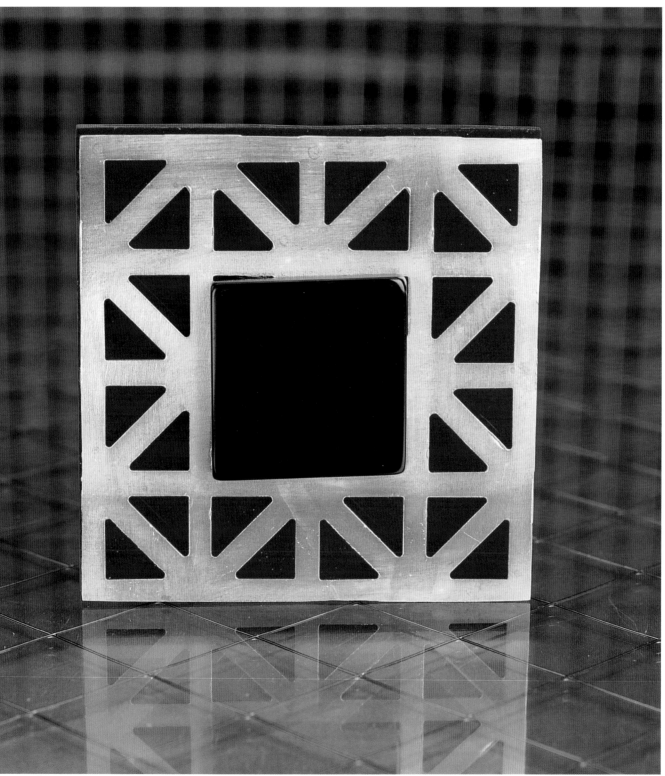

Approximate finished size: 2 ³/₈ inches (6 cm) square and 1 inch (2.5 cm) thick

DUPLEX NECKLACE

This combination of brushed aluminum and brass gives you a good opportunity for working on the technique of creating wire rivets. The secret for successfully turning a short length of wire into a durable connection is patience. You hammer a little on one side, a little on the other, then back to the other.

Tools

- **Jeweler's saw and blades**
- **Bastard file**
- **Flexible shaft with sanding accessories**
- **Sandpaper, 400-grit**
- **Steel ruler**
- **Scribe**
- **Assorted drill bits**
- **Beeswax (optional)**
- **Snips**
- **Chasing hammer**
- **Steel block**
- **Flat-nose pliers**
- **Steel wool, fine grit**

Parts

- **28 inches (71 cm) of aluminum rod, 5 mm**
- **Round brass wire, 18g**
- **Small galvanized or brass nut and bolt**

Assembly

1. Use your saw and blade (a 3/0 blade is best) to cut 14 lengths of the aluminum rod, each 2 inches (5 cm) long. File the ends flush with your bastard file, and then sand the ends.

2. Measure ¼ inch (6 mm) in from one end of each rod section with the ruler, and mark this with the scribe. Measure and mark a spot ¼ inch (6 mm) from the opposite end on each section, making sure that the two marks on each rod are aligned in a parallel line.

3. Use a 1 mm drill bit to drill into the spots marked in step 2. Drill all the way through, keeping your hole centered through the rod. You may want to dip your drill bit in some beeswax for easier drilling.

4. Use the snips to cut 13 lengths of the brass wire, each ½ inch (1.3 cm) long. Make the ends of the pieces flat by either filing with the bastard file or sanding with the flexible shaft attachment and 400-grit sandpaper. If the wire lengths are not straight, gently hammer them on a steel block or use your flat-nose pliers to straighten them out.

5. Insert one length of brass wire into the hole at the end of one aluminum rod section. Place another rod section under the first one with the holes aligned, and continue to thread the brass wire into that hole.

6. Rivet this wire into place, using the steel block and the round end of the chasing hammer. Proceed carefully, and gently hammer one side of the rivet and then turn the pieces over to hammer the other side. Go back and forth until a rivet head has been formed on each side.

7. Rivet together the remaining rod sections in the same way. Arrange the rods as you go so that one rod is on top, the next rod is underneath it, and the following one is on top again. When you've used all 13 wires for the rivet connections, the assembly will have an unattached piece of rod at each end. One unattached end will be from one of the top pieces, and the other a bottom piece.

8. In your flexible shaft, place a drill bit that is at least 1 mm larger than the diameter of the bolt you've chosen for the clasp. With this bit,

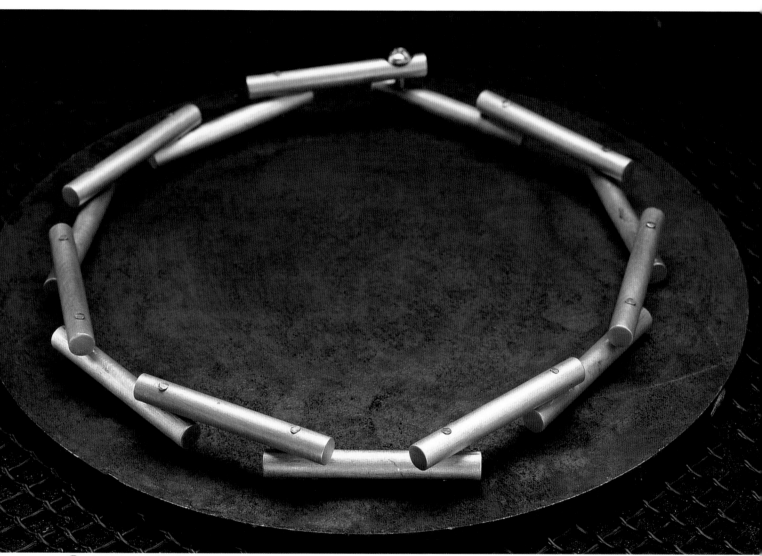

JOANNA GOLLBERG **Approximate finished size:** 19 inches (48.3 cm) around and ½ inch (1.3 cm) thick

enlarge the holes already drilled in the ends of the unattached pieces of aluminum rod. This is where you will insert your nut and bolt to act as the clasp. Insert the nut in the larger hole to make sure it fits correctly, and redrill the hole if necessary. Screw on the bolt to close the clasp.

9. Sand the ends of the rivets until they are smooth and will not scratch anyone wearing the necklace. Use fine-grit steel wool to rub the aluminum back and forth and give it a nice satin finish.

TIP

If the movements between the riveted aluminum rods seem a little too stiff, you can loosen them up a bit by manually moving the sections back and forth at each joint before putting the necklace on.

BEAMING BROOCH

This sunburst of a piece is the first project in the book that requires soldering. As long as you take care to position and angle the silver tubes properly, this should be a fun and easy project to make.

Tools

- **Jeweler's saw and blades**
- **Sandpaper, 400-grit**
- **Measuring tape**
- **Fine-point permanent marker**
- **Round file**
- **Soldering set (see page 40)**
- **T-pins**
- **File**

Parts

- **13 inches (33 cm) of round sterling silver tubing, 4 mm**
- **4 mm round sterling silver tubing in a circle, 1 3/8 inches (3.5 cm) diameter**
- **Pin back finding**

Assembly

1. Cut nine pieces of 4 mm tubing to 1½-inch (3.8 cm) lengths with a jeweler's saw. Smooth the ends of the tubing with sandpaper.

2. Measure around the circle nine equal spaces. A good way to do this is to mark one spot with a permanent marker, and mark two more spots each one-third of the way around the circle. Then mark two spots equally spaced within the thirds for a total of nine.

3. With the round file, file into the tubing circle at each marked spot, creating a small groove on which the straight tubing will rest. File each groove at about a 30° angle from horizontal, with the end of your file that is above the center of the circle up higher than the end on the outside.

4. Place a small amount of soft solder in each groove. Melt the solder into the grooves. Be careful not to use too much—it should barely fill the groove. Pickle the tubing circle.

5. Place a length of tubing on top of the first groove, with ³/₈ inch (9.5 mm) sticking in toward the center of the circle. Let the long end of

the tube rest on your work surface, so that the tube rests on the circle at a slight angle, as shown in Figure 1. If necessary, use a T-pin to secure it in place.

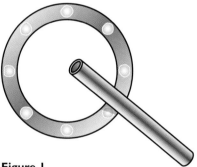

Figure 1

The first straight tube is ready to be soldered to the center circle.

6. Heat the piece until the solder melts and the tube adheres to the circle. Repeat for the other eight straight tubes, making sure that the ends of the tubes all meet evenly to form a circle in the middle. Pickle the whole piece.

7. Solder the pin back to the back of the brooch with soft solder, and then pickle it.

8. File and sand the pin stem.

Approximate finished size: 3½ inches (8.9 cm) in diameter

CHAIN LINK EARRINGS

Made from manufactured jump rings and ear wires, this piece is simplicity itself. The subtle variation of the hammering on the rings enables you to put a personal stamp on it—literally.

Tools

- **Flat-nosed pliers**
- **Soldering set (see page 40)**
- **Medium solder**
- **Planishing hammer**
- **Steel block**
- **Flexible shaft**
- **Silicon burr attachment**
- **Rotary tumbler with steel shot**
- **Burnishing compound**
- **Polishing wheel (optional)**

Parts

- **8 silver jump rings, 16g and 10 mm diameter**
- **Ear wires**

Assembly

1. Attach four of the jump rings to each other, using flat-nosed pliers to close the links.

2. Apply flux to the openings of the jump rings, and solder them closed with medium solder. Then pickle the rings.

3. Hammer each of the links with the more rounded side of the planishing hammer on the steel block, being careful not to hammer on the edge of the block. Vary the hammering to achieve the desired flatness and width of the jump rings.

4. Clean up any burrs left at the soldering points by using a silicon burr on the flexible shaft to grind down burrs both inside and outside of each ring.

5. Tumble the jump rings in the rotary tumbler with steel shot and burnishing compound. Alternately, hand polish the rings carefully on the wheel.

6. Attach an ear wire to one of the end jump rings.

7. Repeat steps 1 though 6 to create the second earring. You may wish to use a polishing wheel to give the earrings a shinier finish.

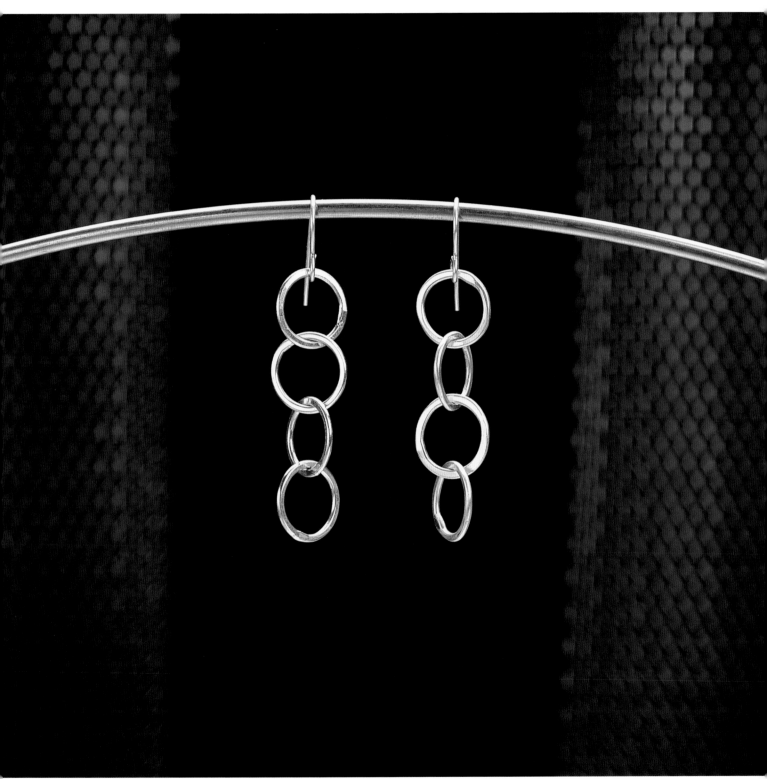

● **EASY**

CONCENTRIC CIRCLES

This set is a symphony of circles. Blackening the silver rings in an oxidizing solution allows the small white pearls dangling at their centers to have an impact much greater than their size would suggest.

NECKLACE & EARRINGS

Tools

- **Steel ruler**
- **Fine-point permanent marker**
- **Round-nose pliers**
- **2 pairs of chain-nose pliers**
- **Safety goggles**
- **Latex gloves**
- **Brass brush**
- **Liquid dish soap**
- **Oxidizing solution**

Parts

- **29 sterling silver balled head pins, 24-gauge, each ½ inch (1.3 cm) long**
- **29 pearls, 4 mm, drilled**
- **21 sterling silver unsoldered jump rings, 18-gauge, with a 4 to 5 mm ID**
- **Sterling silver round wire cable chain, 16 to 18 inches (40.6 to 45.7 cm)**
- **Toggle loop and bar**
- **16-gauge sterling silver soldered jump rings, in the following sizes:**
- **21 pieces with an 8 mm ID**
- **13 pieces with a 15 mm ID**
- **3 pieces with a 22 mm ID**
- **2 ear wires**

Assembly
NECKLACE

1. To ensure that the pearl-drop components are identical, use the fine-point permanent marker to make a mark on the jaws of the round-nose pliers where the jaw diameter is approximately 2 mm. Thread a pearl onto a balled head pin. Holding the end of the pin opposite the pearl at the mark on the jaws, wrap it around the pliers to form a closed loop.

2. Next, gripping the loop near the pearl and opposite the opening, bend the pin away from the opening, in order to center the loop with the axis of the pin.

3. Open all of the 18-gauge jump rings using the two pairs of chain-nose pliers, and set them aside.

4. If you bought a ready-made chain, remove the original clasp by opening the jump rings that hold it in place. Cut through them if they are soldered.

5. Attach the toggle loop to one end of the chain with an open jump ring. Close the jump ring. Attach the toggle bar to the opposite end of the chain using the same method.

6. Wearing safety goggles and latex gloves, clean the 16-gauge soldered jump rings and the chain with a brass brush and soapy water.

7. Dip the pieces in the oxidizing solution until they turn black. Rinse them thoroughly, and dry.

Approximate finished size: 16 x 3 inches (40.6 x 7.6 cm)

CHRISTINE DHEIN

8. The necklace includes six dangle components. To make one dangle, feed an open jump ring through one each of the 8 mm and 15 mm soldered jump rings, as well as through the loop of a pearl component from step 1. Close the jump ring.

9. Feed an open jump ring through one of the 22 mm, 15 mm, and 8 mm soldered jump rings. Add a pearl component. Attach it to the center link on the chain, and then close the jump ring.

10. Using another open jump ring, connect the 22 mm jump ring from step 9 to the 15 mm jump ring of the dangle from step 8. Add an 8 mm jump ring and a pearl component. Close the jump ring.

11. Feed an open jump ring through one of the 8 mm jump rings, a pearl component, and one of the 15 mm jump rings. Attach it to the fourth link from the center of the chain, and close the jump ring. Repeat on the opposite side of the chain to create a symmetrical design.

12. Repeat step 11 to create a dangle for the eighth link from the center of the chain on both sides.

13. Feed an open jump ring through a 15 mm jump ring, an 8 mm jump ring, and a pearl component. Attach it to the 12th link from the center, and close the jump ring. Repeat on the opposite side of the chain for symmetry.

14. To decorate the clasp, feed an open jump ring through a pearl component, an 8 mm jump ring, and a 15 mm jump ring to create a dangle. Attach it to the clasp itself or to a link in the chain next to the clasp. Close the jump ring.

15. Open the loop of eight of the remaining pearl components. Feed one onto the bottom 8 mm jump ring of each dangle on the necklace, and then secure it by closing the loop.

Approximate finished size: 2¼ x 1 inch (5.7 x 2.5 cm)

EARRINGS

16. The earrings are made of different dangle components than the necklace. Create two dangles by feeding an open 18-gauge jump ring through one 15 mm jump ring, two 8 mm jump rings, and a pearl component. Close the jump ring.

17. Feed another open 18-gauge jump ring through a pearl component, a 22 mm, 15 mm, and 8 mm jump ring, and the 15 mm jump ring of the earring dangle. Close the jump ring.

18. Repeat steps 16 and 17 to create the second earring.

19. Open the loops of the ear wires. Feed a pearl and the 8 mm jump ring at the top of one dangle onto the loop of an ear wire, and close. Repeat to complete the second earring.

● **EASY**

GEOMETRY NECKLACE

Geometry might be difficult to master in school, but not in making this set of pieces. Ready-made silver shapes are easily combined with chains, hoops, and jump rings into an attractive design.

● **AMY TAVERN**

Tools

- Chasing hammer
- Steel block
- 2 pairs of needle- or flat-nose pliers

Parts

- Ready-made sterling silver circles and squares in varying sizes from ½ to 1½ inches (1.3 to 3.8 cm) in diameter
- 2 commercial 1.1 mm sterling silver cable chains, 16 inches (40.6 cm) long each
- 2 commercial sterling silver hoop earrings
- 2 sterling silver jump rings, 5 mm and 20-gauge

TIP

As with the earrings, this necklace can be worn in many different combinations, using both chains or, for a shorter necklace, only one chain.

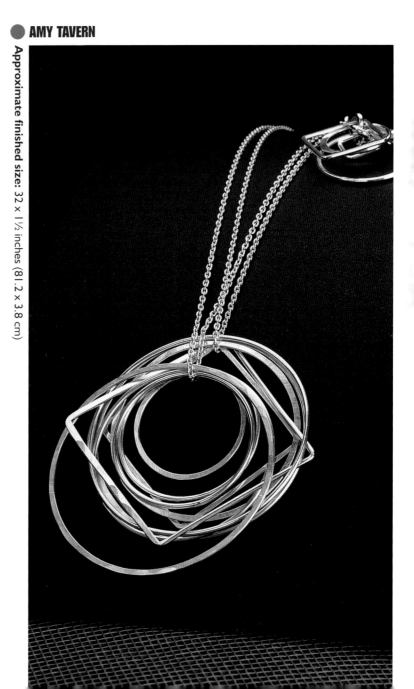

Approximate finished size: 32 × 1½ inches (81.2 × 3.8 cm)

Assembly

NECKLACE

1. First, set aside two of each size of the ready-made silver circles and squares that you have. These will be used for the earrings.

2. Using the flat side of a chasing hammer and a steel block, lightly hammer each remaining circle and square to create a flattened, multifaceted surface. For each piece, start hammering at one point on the shape and follow the surface in one direction until you reach your starting point. To create a different look for each piece, you can instead hammer halfway around or only in various points.

3. To assemble the necklace: Thread a small circle onto the clasp of one cable chain, and hook the two chains together.

4. Thread the rest of the hammered shapes onto the combined chains.

5. Choose a square and one or two other shapes to hook in the other clasp, and hook the clasps together.

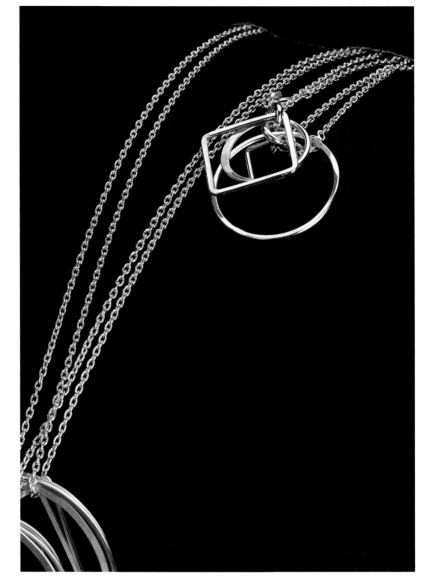

The clasp of the necklace also includes an assortment of geometric shapes.

EARRINGS

6. To make the earrings, take one of each size of the circle and square shapes you set aside earlier. Just as in step 2, lightly hammer each piece to make flatter, multifaceted surfaces. Take the matching piece in each size and shape you set aside, and hammer those as well. Be sure to do the same treatment on matching parts—that is, one 1-inch (2.5 cm) square should closely resemble the other 1-inch (2.5 cm) square. When you're done, you should have two matching sets of circles and squares.

7. Open one jump ring with pliers and use it to hook two shapes together, then close the jump ring. In the example shown here, the jump rings connect a 1-inch (2.5 cm) square with a ¾-inch (1.9 cm) circle. Repeat this step with the other jump ring and a matching pair of shapes.

8. Thread one set of hammered shapes onto one hoop earring, including one of the two linked shapes (here, it's the 1-inch [2.5 cm] square), and repeat for the other earring.

9. These earrings can be worn in endless combinations using as many or as few of the shapes as you like.

Approximate finished size: 3¼ x 1½ inches (8.3 x 3.8 cm)

Approximate finished size: 1½ x ¾ x ¼ inches (3.8 x 1.9 cm x 6 mm)

 **JOANNA GOLLBERG**

BRASS ORB RING

The tiny jump rings that come already attached to the three brass balls make this piece easier to construct, and they allow for plenty of movement (and even a little sound) when it is worn. This is not a good piece to wear if you want to sneak up on anyone.

Tools

- **Snips**
- **Chain-nose pliers**
- **Steel wool, heavy grit**
- **Soldering set (see page 40)**

Parts

- **Sterling silver jump ring, 18g and 5 mm diameter**
- **2 brass balls with an attached jump ring, 7 mm**
- **Brass ball with an attached jump ring, 10 mm**
- **Sterling silver band ring, 5 mm wide and 2 mm thick (ring size of your choice)**

Assembly

1. Use the snips to cut the 5 mm jump ring in half. Keep one half, and put the other aside (you will not need it for this project).

2. Use the chain-nose pliers to squeeze the half jump ring together so it forms a tight "U" shape.

3. Use the heavy-grit steel wool to give the three brass balls a shiny finish.

4. Using hard solder and the soldering equipment, solder one end of the U-shaped jump ring to the middle of the ring band's outer surface. Pickle the piece, and then rinse it.

5. Open the jump ring with the chain-nose pliers enough to slide the brass balls onto the "U." Thread on one 7 mm ball, the 10 mm ball, and then the other 7 mm ball.

6. Use the chain-nose pliers to close the unsoldered end of the jump ring, making sure the end of the "U" touches the ring band.

7. Solder the remaining end of the "U" onto the ring band with easy solder. Pickle the piece and rinse when done.

8. Give the ring a final finish by rubbing it with the heavy-grit steel wool.

Approximate finished size: 18 x 2 inches (45.7 x 5 cm)

● **TONYA MOORE**

● **EASY**

SHADOW NECKLACE

A typical job for a cotter pin like those dangling here is to hold a wheel on an axle, or to keep one of a teddy bear's joints together. Browse through a hardware store with an open mind, and you're likely to find other components you can turn from functional to decorative.

Tools

- Flat glass surface
- Wire cutters
- File
- 2 pairs of flat-nose pliers
- Soldering set (see page 40)
- Half-round needle file
- Scribe
- Third-hand cross-locking tweezers
- 2-inch (5 cm) nail
- Vise
- Extra wire
- Sandpaper, 400- and 800-grit
- Dish soap
- Tumbler and shot
- Soft cloth

FACT

Why is one side of a cotter pin longer than the other? It's to make it easier to bend back one side first when you need to keep the pin in place. That's something you won't be doing in this project, but it could help the next time you have a wheel to fix.

Parts

- 2 cotter pins, 2 inches (5 cm) long
- 4 cotter pins, $1^{7}/_{8}$ inches (4.7 cm) long
- 12 cotter pins, $1^{3}/_{8}$ inches (3.5 cm) long
- Black shiny car enamel spray paint
- 1-inch (2.5 cm) length of 16-gauge sterling silver wire
- 20 jump rings, 4 mm and 16-gauge
- 32 jump rings, 7 mm and 16-gauge
- 10 jump rings, 12 mm and 16-gauge

Assembly

1. Place all the cotter pins on a flat piece of glass resting on a flat surface. Spray evenly with black shiny car enamel, being careful not to make any puddles. Let the first coat dry and then apply two more light coats, making sure to let each coat dry completely before continuing. Flip the cotter pins over and repeat with three coats of paint on the other side.

2. File each end of the sterling silver wire evenly, and then set it aside.

3. Using two pairs of flat-nose pliers, close three of the 4 mm jump rings so that the ends overlap, and then pull them back apart slightly and twist the ends together so they line up tightly. Solder the jump rings closed. Use the half-round needle file to file a small flat area on the rings opposite the solder joint.

4. Solder two of the jump rings from step 3 onto opposite ends of

63

the 16-gauge sterling wire. This will be the toggle for your clasp. Measure ½ inch (1.3 cm) across the toggle and mark it with a scribe. Solder the last jump ring here. This is where the necklace will join the toggle.

5. Divide the thirty-two 7 mm jump rings into eight groups of four. Link and close each group, using the two flat-nose pliers. Solder the ends of the linked jump rings closed. Repeat until you have created eight chains. Then place each link in turn in the third-hand tweezers. Apply a small amount of flux and a small snippet of solder across the joint. Heat the jump ring from below with the torch until the solder melts and flows into the joint. After you're done with all 32 jump rings, pickle and rinse the chains.

6. Link two of the chains together with one of the 12 mm jump rings, and close the ring to seal it. Don't solder it yet. Repeat to create three more chains from the six shorter chains remaining. Join two of the longer chains with another 12 mm jump ring, and close the ring to seal it. Repeat to link the other two chains. You should have two chains now.

7. Link these two lengths together by adding a 12 mm jump ring onto one end of each chain. Then attach three 4 mm jump rings in a row to each of the two 12 mm rings just added. Link the two chains together by connecting another 12 mm jump ring to the last 4 mm ring on each chain. You should have one long chain now.

8. On one end of the chain, link eight 4 mm jump rings and the toggle. Solder each of the 4 mm jump rings closed.

9. Close and solder the 12 mm jump ring closest to the toggle. Skip the next two 12 mm jump rings, as

these will hold cotter pins and will not be soldered because the heat from the torch would destroy the car enamel. Close and solder the fourth 12 mm jump ring from the toggle, and solder the three 4 mm jump rings that follow. Skip the next 12 mm jump ring, but solder the three 4 mm jump rings after it and the next 12 mm jump ring. Skip the next two 12 mm jump rings, but solder the last 12 mm jump ring.

10. To the non-toggle end of the necklace, add three more 4 mm jump rings and a 12 mm jump ring. Solder the rings closed. The toggle will attach to this last 12 mm ring. When done, pickle and rinse the chain.

11. Place the nail in the vise at an angle. Make a loop with a scrap piece of wire at the end of the chain. Fasten the loop over the nail, and pull the chain straight with one hand. With your other hand, sand the chain with the 400-grit sandpaper along the entire length. When you've completely sanded all sides of the chain, switch to 800-grit sandpaper, and repeat. When you're done sanding, remove the chain from the nail, remove the wire loop, and wash the chain with some dish soap, removing any grit.

12. Place the chain in the tumbler, and cover it with about ¾ inch (1.9 cm) of shot. Add 2½ inches (6.4 cm) of water and a teaspoon (5 mL) of dish soap. Tumble for at least 2½ hours. When you remove the chain from the tumbler, it should be shiny. Dry it with the soft cloth or a T-shirt.

13. Next, add the painted cotter pins in different lengths to the 12 mm jump rings that you didn't solder together. On the project pictured here, each jump ring holds five cotter pins. Make sure the cotter pins are all facing in the same direction. Close all unsoldered jump rings with the two pairs of flat-nose pliers, making sure the joints fit snugly.

XYLOPHONE PENDANT

When making this jazzy piece, you have room for improvisation, as the lines and patterns scratched on the painted tubes are entirely up to you. Whatever designs you choose, the shiny aluminum peeking through the black will go well with the silver chain and dividers.

Tools

- Jeweler's saw and blades
- Tube-cutting jig (optional)
- Bastard file
- Sandpaper, 400-grit
- Flexible shaft with sanding attachment
- Scribe
- Dividers
- Assorted drill bits
- Scrap wire or string
- Steel ruler
- Soldering set (see page 40)
- Snips
- Steel wool, very fine grit

Parts

- Aluminum tubing, 8 mm ID, 10 mm OD
- Sterling silver tubing, 2.2 mm ID, 2.5 mm OD
- 30 inches (76.2 cm) of silver snake chain, 2.5 mm
- Spray paint, black glossy enamel

Approximate finished size: 14 x 2¾ inches (35.6 cm x 7 cm)

● JOANNA GOLLBERG

65

Assembly

1. Using your saw and a relatively coarse blade such as a 3/0, cut five pieces of the aluminum tubing in lengths that vary from 2¼ to 2¾ inches (5.7 to 7 cm). The tubing should be cut at a right angle to its length, so use a tube-cutting jig if you have one.

2. File the ends of the tubing smooth with the bastard file. Remove any remaining burrs by sanding with 400-grit sandpaper in a flexible shaft sanding attachment.

3. Use your scribe to gently draw a line down the length of each piece of tubing.

4. Open your dividers to a width of 1 inch (2.5 cm). Lay out the five sections of tubing in the order you'd like them in the finished piece, with the line you drew in step 3 facing up. Use the dividers to mark two short lines on each piece of tubing across the horizontal line. Those lines, all 1 inch (2.5 cm) apart, should line up vertically on all five tubing pieces, as shown in figure 1.

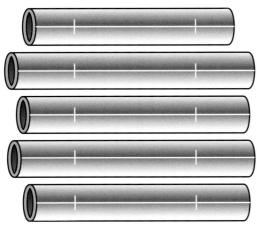

Figure 1

The spots for drilling holes in the tubes form two parallel lines.

5. With the flexible shaft and a 2.2 mm drill bit, drill holes at the two places on each tube where the long scribed line is crossed by the divider lines. If you initially have trouble drilling the 2.2 mm holes, you can first drill holes with a 1 mm drill bit. This will give you a smaller pilot hole to help guide the larger drill bit.

6. After drilling two holes on the top of each piece of tubing, drill again through each hole until you hit the bottom part of the tubing. Be sure to drill straight through at a 90° angle to the opposite side of the tubing. You will now have four holes in each piece.

7. Hang the tubing pieces on a piece of wire or string so that the tubing does not touch the ground. You can either thread the wire or string through the length of the tubing pieces, or put it through the two holes at one end of each tube and let the pieces dangle. Spray each piece of tubing with the black paint until the outsides of the tubes are covered completely. Let the paint dry.

8. With your scribe, scratch off lines, shapes, or small areas on the black spray paint in whatever design you choose.

9. To make spacers for between the long tubes, cut 12 lengths of the silver tubing with your saw, each ¼ inch (6 mm) long. Sand the ends of these spacers until they are smooth and as even in length as possible.

10. Flux the inside of two of the spacers. With the pair of snips, cut two lengths of easy solder approximately ⅛ inch (3 mm) long. Place one of these solder pallions inside each of the two spacers, and melt them with your torch. Pickle the two spacers, and rinse.

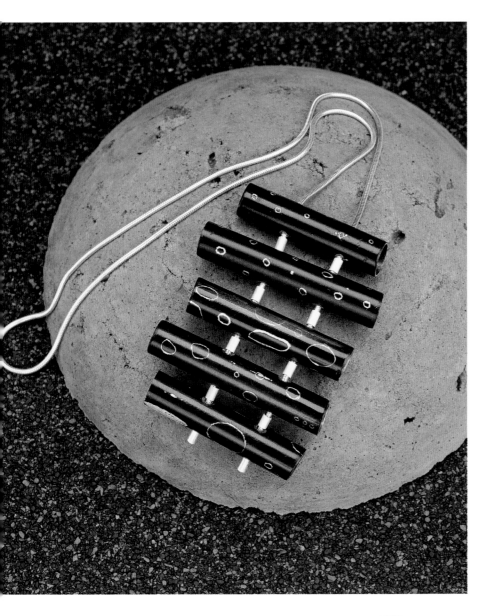

11. To assemble the piece, first thread each end of the snake chain through the top holes of the black tube you've chosen as the top one. Thread the chain ends through the spacers and the other four black tubes in the desired order until the ends are coming through the bottom holes on the bottom tube.

12. Flux the inside of the two spacers from step 10 with a small amount of flux. Thread these spacers onto the two ends of the snake chain, making sure the chain does not poke out of the end of the spacers.

13. Before soldering, move the black tubes with the other spacers as far away up the chain from the two chain ends as possible. (This is to avoid any heat damage to the painted aluminum.) With a very gentle torch flame, reheat the spacers with the solder melted inside. Keep the flame angled away from the chain, but toward the end of the spacers; this is so you won't melt or solder the chain to itself. Pickle and then rinse the ends of the chain.

14. Finish the end spacers by rubbing them with the very fine grit steel wool.

PILLAR NECKLACE & EARRINGS

Working with a limited number of shapes and colors doesn't require limiting your creativity. Making this matched set, you can play with shapes (round, square, rectangle, and oval), color (silver and copper), and a variety of lengths to end with a striking effect.

Tools

- Jeweler's saw and blades
- Silver paste solder
- Jeweler's torch with a small tip
- Sturdy metal nippers (optional)
- Fine-point permanent marking pen
- Center punch
- Flexible shaft
- Drill bit, 1 mm size
- Small jeweler's hammer
- Steel block
- Needle file
- Soldering set (see page 40)
- Fine-grit rubber wheel attachment
- Binding or scrap wire
- Finishing material, such as fine steel wool, very fine sandpaper, or fiberglass pen
- Flat-nose pliers

Parts

- Round sterling silver tubing, 6 mm
- Square sterling silver tubing, 5 mm
- Oval sterling silver tubing, 4 x 6 mm
- Round copper tubing, 4 mm
- Square copper rod, 2 mm
- Round copper rod, 2 mm
- Rectangle sterling silver wire, 1 x 3 mm
- 17 inches (43.2 cm) of commercial sterling cable neck wire with unfinished clasp ends
- 1 pair of commercial sterling silver wire beading hoop earrings, 22-gauge and 19 mm diameter

Part Preparation
NECKLACE & EARRINGS

1. Using the jeweler's saw, cut several 2 to 3 mm slices from each piece of tubing and rod. Note: this does not include the rectangle sterling silver wire.

2. Arrange the slices of tubes and rods in combinations of two slices each, similar to those in the necklace and earrings shown here. You can put small slices within or outside larger ones, match up or contrast solid and hollow shapes, combine or separate silver and copper—whatever you'd like. Then place the paste solder between the slices in the spots where you want to join them. Heat with the torch until the pieces are joined.

3. Using the saw or the pair of nippers, cut the rectangle wire in 30 pieces, varying the lengths from about 1/3 to 1 inch (8 mm to 2.5 cm).

Approximate finished size: **Necklace** 17 x 1½ inches (43.2 x 3.8 cm); **Earrings** 1½ inches (3.8 cm) long

● **RAMSEY HALL**

Assembly

NECKLACE

4. Lay 16 to 18 pieces flat, arranging them side by side in alternating lengths, as shown in figure 1. Choose three of the longer pieces to be attached to the tube pieces.

5. Lay the neck wire across the pieces. Dot each piece with the permanent marking pen adjacent to the wire; some pieces should have a dot near the middle, and others closer to one end or the other. Number each piece in order with the marking pen. Put an X on the three pieces that will be soldered to tubing-and-rod slices.

6. Center punch and drill each piece at the dots. Make sure the hole is a little larger than your neck wire.

7. Using the small hammer and the steel block, lightly texture the narrow surface of the rectangle pieces.

8. Flush file one end of each of the three "X" pieces, and solder one tubing-and-rod combination to each. File the ends of the other rectangle pieces, then smooth the ends with the fine-grit rubber wheel inserted into the flexible shaft.

9. Thread all the pieces, by number, onto the piece of binding or scrap wire, and loop the ends so they won't slide off. Now you can clean and finish the pieces in your preferred manner. (Fine steel wool, very fine sandpaper, or the fiberglass pen all work well here.)

10. Remove the finished pieces from the scrap wire, and thread them in the same order onto the neck wire. Crimp the clasp part onto the unfinished end of the neck wire.

EARRINGS

11. You make the earrings in the same manner as the necklace, beginning with step 4 and continuing through step 9. The differences are that you use only 5 to 7 rectangle pieces for each earring, and only one longer piece on each earring is marked for attaching pieces of tubing and rods.

12. To complete the earrings, thread the finished pieces in order onto the hoops.

TIP

You can make and finish all the pieces for the necklace and earrings (steps 4 through 9) at the same time. That way, you won't have to go back to do the same tasks (drilling, filing, and so on) at two different times. Just make sure you keep track of which pieces belong with the necklace and with each earring.

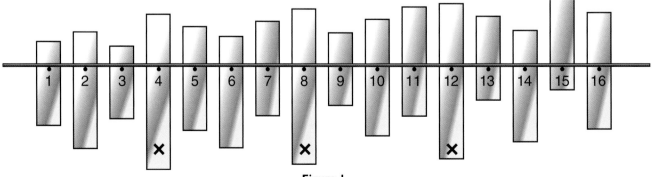

Figure 1
As you arrange the "pillars" of the necklace, vary the length of the pieces and the position of the holes.

ORBIT CUFF

This combination of circles is simple in its construction, with only two different parts and one technique—soldering—employed in its creation. Visually, though, the coppery discs, which almost seem to be floating, and the various angles of the thin rings you bend by hand give the piece a more complicated and intriguing look.

Tools

- **Soldering set (see page 40)**
- **Liver of sulfur**
- **Steel wool, coarse grit**

Parts

- **5 brass bangle blanks, 2 mm square wire and 2¾ inches (7 cm) diameter**
- **8 brass round disks, 24g and ½ inch (1.3 cm) diameter**

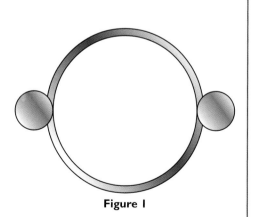

Figure 1

Solder two discs on top of four of the bangles as shown.

Assembly

1. With four of the bangles, solder two disks on top of each bangle, using hard solder. The two disks should be located directly opposite each other, and the edge of each disk should be flush with the inside edge of the bangle, as in figure 1. Pickle and rinse the soldered pieces.

2. Neatly stack the four soldered bangles with the disks facing up. The eight disks should be spaced an even distance from one another around the outside of the stack. Place the fifth bangle on top of the stack

3. Use easy solder to solder each disk to the bangle on top of it. As you did in step 1, align the edge of each disc flush with the inside edge of the bangle you're soldering it to. Pickle and rinse.

4. Use your fingers to pry apart the bangles and create spaces in between them. To do this, grasp two adjacent bangles, one with each hand, at a spot that is not near any soldered disk. Gently pull the two bangles away from each other at that spot. Work your way around the bracelet until the bangles only touch one another at the disk positions. At other points, the bangles will be separated by gaps of about ¼ inch (6 mm) or a little more.

5. Place a chunk of the liver of sulfur in a glass bowl with some hot water until it has dissolved completely. Place the bracelet in the solution until the brass turns a darker color. This will probably not be an extremely dark patina, as liver of sulfur will not completely blacken brass. Rinse the bracelet in water.

6. Use the coarse-grit steel wool to rub off any areas of the patina where you do not want a darker color. Continue rubbing with the steel wool on the areas of the bracelet that you want to be shiny.

Approximate finished size: 3³/₄ x 1¹/₂ inches (9.5 x 3.8 cm)

● **JOANNA GOLLBERG**

SILHOUETTE BRACELET

The number of ways you can combine different geometrical shapes within the six squares of this piece must be astronomical. Its smart design—notice the clever clasp—is composed entirely of tubing and jump rings.

Tools

- Sandpaper, 400-grit
- Dividers
- Jeweler's saw and blades
- Tube-cutting jig
- Soldering set (see page 40)
- Two pairs of needle-nose pliers
- Liver of sulfur
- Brass brush (optional)
- Tumbler, ceramic or plastic shot, and polishing compound (optional)

Parts

- Square metal tubing, 19 mm
- Metal tubing in various shapes (round, square, triangle) and sizes (5 to 13 mm)
- Round metal tubing, 5 mm
- Square metal tubing, 3 mm
  - 6 or 7 jump rings, 18g and 7 mm
  - 2 or 3 small jump rings (approximately 18g and 5 mm)

Assembly

1. To prepare the various pieces of tubing for cutting, first sand the ends of the tubes on a flat surface until each is flat and even.

2. Set your dividers to a width of 5 mm, then lightly mark all the way around the tube with the dividers. Use that line as your guide while sawing through the tube with the jeweler's saw. If the tubing is smaller than 6 mm in diameter, hold it in place with the tube-cutting jig while sawing. For thicker tubing, saw carefully along your marked line.

3. Choosing from among the 5 to 13 mm tubes, you can decide how many slices of each shape and size to place within the largest squares of the bracelet. (One limit to your creativity here: the clasp-holding end square must have only one large square within it for the clasp to work properly.) The bracelet pictured here, for example, has within its six linked squares these shapes: one large square, two medium squares, three medium circles, and one each of a small square, circle, and triangle. After sawing each piece that you decide to include, sand the newly cut slice on the flat surface and set it aside. Before cutting another piece from the same tube, sand the end of the tubing flat as you did in step 2.

4. Cut 11 pieces of the 5 mm round tubing. Sand them and set them aside for soldering on the sides of the squares.

5. Once all of the tubing pieces have been cut and sanded, lay out the bracelet pieces on a soldering block. Set up the six large squares in a row with one or two (or perhaps three small) shapes inside each. For five of the large squares, place two 5 mm round tubing pieces on the outside of each; these two pieces should be centered on opposite sides of the square. The sixth square (an end square) will be the clasp holder; for that square, place a 12 or 13 mm square within it on one side, and just one 5 mm round ring outside the opposite side.

6. Lightly apply wet flux along all of the areas where the tubing pieces intersect, and solder together with medium solder.

7. Once you have all of the components for the bracelet completed and pickled, sand both sides flat, and polish to remove any sharp edges.

8. To make the toggle end of the clasp, cut a piece of 3 mm square tubing about 1 inch (2.5 cm) long, and fine sand the ends.

9. Join one of the 7 mm jump rings to the round tubing piece on the outside of an end square component; this will be the large square that is at the opposite end of the bracelet from the square with only one tubing piece and one large interior square (see the detail photo). Attach this jump ring to two or three 5 mm jump rings in a chain. Solder all the jump ring links closed, then solder the final jump ring in the chain to the center of the square tubing piece from step 8.

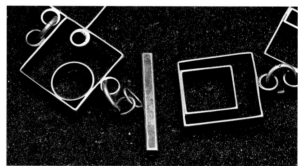

Just right: The interior square at one end of the bracelet needs to be big enough for the "toggle bar" clasp to slip inside it easily, but not so big that the bar will slip out as the bracelet is worn.

10. Join the other large square components with the other 7 mm jump rings. Solder the rings closed, and pickle the bracelet. Gently sandpaper off any burrs or sharp edges.

11. To oxidize the bracelet, dissolve a tiny piece of the liver of sulfur in hot water, and soak the bracelet. You can leave the metal black by brass brushing and waxing it. To get the more marbled finish shown here, put the blackened bracelet in a vibratory tumbler with ceramic or plastic shot and burnishing compound.

ATOMIC EARRINGS

The silvery globes drilled with a variety of pinpoint holes may remind you of a number of things—if not an atom, then perhaps a planet, or even a childhood visit to a planetarium. In any case, something about these earrings suggests a vision of the future taken from the past.

Tools

- **Assorted drill bits (suggested sizes: #72, #58, #65)**
- **Flexible shaft**
- **Sanding sticks in 220-, 400-, and 600-grit, or scrubbing-pad wheel attachment for flexible shaft**
- **Tube-cutting jig**
- **Steel ruler**
- **Jeweler's saw and blades**
- **Round ball burr attachment**
- **Soldering set (see page 40)**
- **Third hand tweezers**
- **Heat shield compound**
- **Pickle**
- **Flat-nose pliers**
- **Polishing cloth**

Parts

- **2 sterling silver ball beads, 16 mm diameter**
- **4 sterling silver ball beads, 6 mm diameter**
- **3-inch (7.6 cm) length of 2.5 mm sterling silver round tubing**
- **2 ear posts**
- **2 ear nuts**

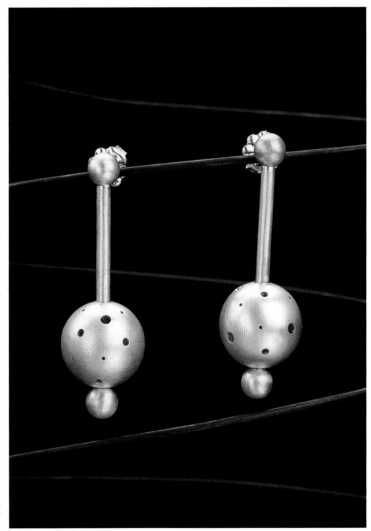

Approximate finished size: 3¼ x 1½ inches (8.3 x 3.8 cm)

● **KRISTIN LORA**

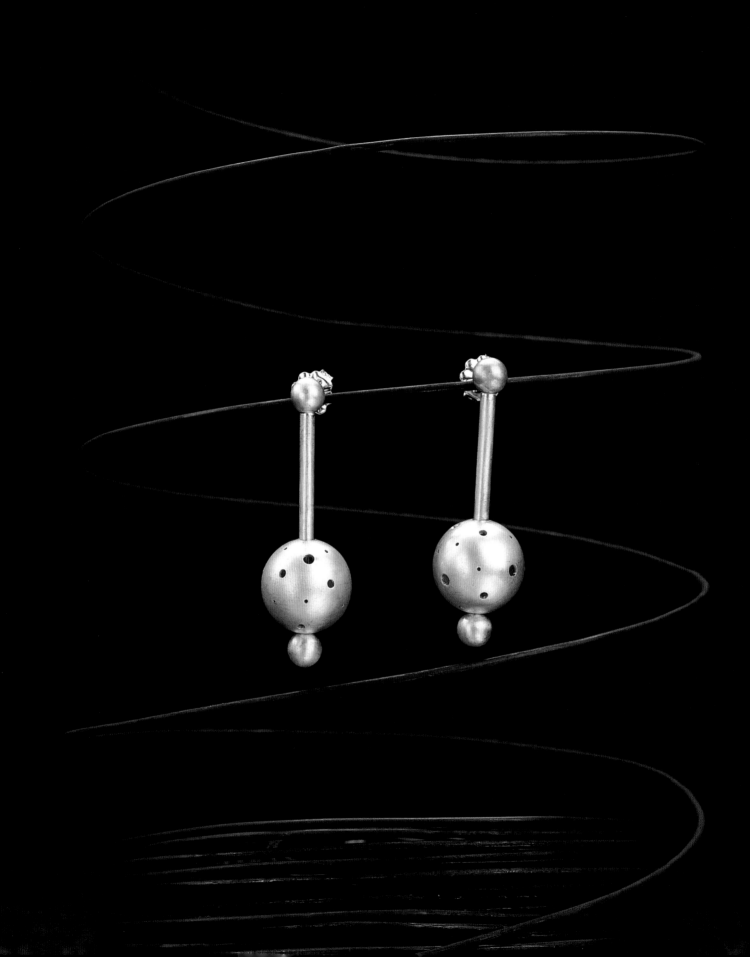

Assembly

1. Using a very small drill bit (such as a #72) in the flexible shaft, drill random holes all around the two 16 mm ball beads. Randomly enlarge several of the holes with the #58 drill bit and several others with the #65 drill bit, leaving some holes at the smallest size. Use the sanding sticks (going from lowest number grit to highest) or the scrubbing-pad wheel to remove any burrs.

2. Try to slide the piece of round tubing through the two original holes at each end of the 16 mm ball beads. If the tubing doesn't fit, use a drill bit that will enlarge the holes just enough for the tubing to slide through.

3. Using the tube-cutting jig and the steel ruler, measure and cut the tubing to make two pieces that are 1½ inches (3.8 cm) long. With the round ball burr in the flexible shaft, finish the two ends of each piece of tubing so that a 6 mm round bead will sit just inside each end.

4. Solder one 6 mm bead on the end of each tube piece with the open hole facing up.

5. Slide one of the 16 mm beads onto one of the tubes until it is next to the already soldered ball end. Secure the tube upright in the third hand, and solder one 6 mm bead on the other end. Do the same with the other tube and 16 mm ball bead.

6. Apply some heat shield compound around the base of where the 6 mm bead attaches to the tubing. Carefully solder one ear post to the side of one of the 6 mm beads on each earring, placing the post perpendicular to the tubing.

7. After pickling the pieces, twist the two ear posts with flat-nose pliers to work-harden them, then polish the earrings and put on the ear nuts.

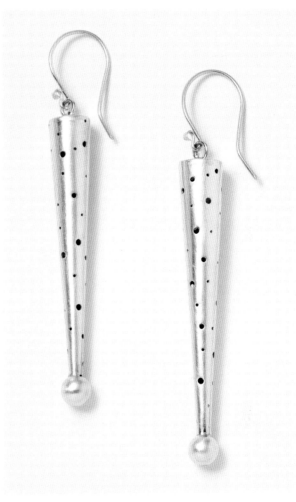

This pair of earrings by Kristin Lora features techniques and materials similar to those used in the Atomic Earrings, though the different shapes used give it a very different effect.

BUNDLES BRACELET

Here you cut rectangular tubing to just two different lengths and combine the pieces with standardized stampings and jump rings into a simple and elegant design. The bundles of twisty wires with balled ends add a natural touch to the geometric composition.

Tools

- **Calipers**
- **Scribe**
- **Needle files**
- **Jeweler's saw and blades**
- **Soldering set (see page 40)**
- **Third-hand tweezers**
- **Nail**
- **Vise**
- **Sandpaper, 400- and 800-grit**
- **Tumbler and shot**
- **Liquid dish soap**
- **Flat-nose pliers**

Parts

- **Rectangular silver tubing, 2.9 x 1.7 mm (.117 x .067 inch)**
- **16-gauge jump rings, 4 mm**
- **22-gauge round wire**
- **26-gauge rectangle sterling silver stampings, 13 x 5 mm (.5 x .2 inches)**
- **16-gauge jump rings, 7 mm**
- **16-gauge jump rings, 12 mm**
- **Ready-made ear posts**

Assembly

BRACELET

1. With the calipers and the scribe, mark 24 pieces of rectangular tubing to 3 mm lengths. Cut out each 3 mm piece carefully on the scribe line, and file the edges flat with a needle file. Next, mark six 8 mm pieces of tubing in the same way, cut to length, and file the edges.

2. Measure out a ¾-inch (1.9 cm) piece of the tubing, cut it, and file its edges smooth. Measure 8 mm in from one end and mark with the scribe. Close and solder one of the 4 mm jump rings. File a smooth edge on the jump ring on the opposite side of the solder joint. Solder the jump ring onto the 8 mm mark of the ¾-inch (1.9 cm) piece of tubing. This is the bracelet's toggle.

3. With the scribe, mark each 8 mm piece of tubing 4 mm down from top. Solder a 3 mm piece of tubing on both sides of the 4 mm mark on all six pieces of 8 mm tubing (see figure 1).

Two tubes of 3 mm length are soldered to each 8 mm tube.

Figure 1

4. Thread through all six 8 mm pieces of tubing with five to six pieces of 22-gauge wire cut into various lengths. Fill each piece with wire until you can't force

 **TONYA MOORE**   **Approximate finished size: Bracelet** 7½ inches (19 cm) long; **Earrings** 1½ x 1 x ⅛ inch (3.8 x 2.5 cm x 3 mm)

anymore into the tubing. Next, ball up each end of the round wire with the torch. Then thread five to six pieces of the round wire of various lengths into the ¾-inch (1.9 cm) tubing. Ball up all ends of round wire with the torch.

5. Lay out five rectangle stampings horizontally and lengthwise on your soldering block. Mark all five stampings 2 mm up from the bottom on both vertical sides. Solder a 3 mm piece of tubing to each side of the rectangles at this marking (see figure 2). A good way to do this is to place the rectangle vertically in third-hand tweezers. Hold a 3 mm piece of tubing on top of the rectangle with another third hand at the 2 mm mark. Flux and solder at the joint.

Two tubes of 3 mm length are soldered to the ends of five of the rectangle stampings.

Figure 2

6. On two more rectangles, mark 2 mm up on only one side of each (see figure 3). Solder a 3 mm piece of square tubing on each of these marks. Pickle and rinse all pieces that have been soldered.

Two stampings have only one 3 mm tube attached.

Figure 3

7. Next, using the five rectangles that have tubing soldered onto both sides (from step 5), thread three of the pieces of tubing with a 7 mm jump ring on each side. Do not close the jump rings. Link one rectangle with jump rings attached and link through one open end of the three-piece tubing assemblies (from step 3) with balled round wire. Link another triple tubing link on the other side of the rectangle. Attach the next rectangle onto the triple link end, and add another triple link end to the rectangle. Attach the next rectangle and then another triple tubing link.

8. Using the last two rectangles, thread one of the tubes on each rectangle with 7 mm jump rings. Thread the other tubing on each rectangle with 4 mm jump rings. Attach each rectangle to triple-tubing assemblies on opposite ends of the chain by the 7 mm jump rings. Next, attach three 4 mm jump rings to each end of the bracelet. On the left side of the bracelet attach a 12 mm jump ring, and on the right side attach the toggle.

9. Using third-hand tweezers to hold each jump ring in the bracelet, solder all joints. Pickle the bracelet, rinse, and pat dry.

10. Place the nail in the vise at an angle. Make a loop out of extra wire, and attach it to the jump-ring end of the bracelet. Hook the loop over the nail, and pull the bracelet out straight with your hand. Use your other hand to rub 400-grit sandpaper lengthwise over both sides of the bracelet. Switch to 800-grit paper, and repeat. Rinse the bracelet with dish soap, making sure to remove all grit. Place it in a tumbler filled with ¾ inch (1.9 cm) of shot and 2½ inches (6.4 cm) of water with 1 teaspoon (5 mL) of dish soap. Tumble for at least two hours, then dry the bracelet with a soft T-shirt when finished.

EARRINGS

11. Using the two remaining rectangles with only one piece of tubing soldered to them, lay them out vertically lengthwise. The tubing should be on the bottom. Next, use a 7 mm jump ring to attach each rectangle link to a triple tubing link. To complete the earrings, add a 12 mm jump ring to each triple tubing link on each earring. Close and solder all jump rings.

12. Mark the back of each rectangle stamping in the earrings 1 mm down and 2 mm across. Solder a ready-made ear post to each earring. Pickle and rinse the earrings. Sand them with 400- and then 800-grit sandpaper. Wash with dish soap and rinse. Place the earrings in the tumbler (prepared as in step 10) for two hours. Dry them with a soft T-shirt.

CERULEAN NECKLACE

The golden edges of this piece, seemingly worn by time, bring an echo of ancient Rome to these metal disks that you can find at your local hardware store.

Tools

- Fine-point permanent marker
- Flexible shaft
- Drill bit, 1.5 mm
- Small-hair paintbrush
- Soft cotton cloth
- Snips
- Flat- and chain-nose pliers
- Soldering set (see page 40)
- 14k easy solder
- Brass brush

Parts

- 8 round galvanized steel washers, 1³/₈ inches (3.5 cm) outside diameter
- Blue shimmering car spray paint
- Gold leaf and gold leaf fixative glue (available at large craft stores)
- 18 inches of 14k gold-filled curb chain, 2 mm
- 10 14k gold-filled wire jump rings, 20g and 3 mm
- 14k gold-plated commercial spring clasp

Assembly

1. Mark and drill two holes in each washer, one hole at 10 o'clock and one at 2 o'clock, each ¹/₈ inch (3 mm) away from the edge of the washer.

2. Put down some newspaper to protect your surface, and spray paint each of the washers with the blue spray paint. Be sure to spray outside or in a well-ventilated area. Paint one side of the washers, and let them dry. Then turn them over and spray the other side, making sure to cover the washers completely with paint.

3. After the paint dries, use the small-hair paintbrush to paint on gold leaf fixative glue in small areas on one side of each washer. You can add more gold leaf or less to suit your taste. Follow the instructions on the fixative before applying the gold leaf.

4. Rinse the brush you used for the gold leaf fixative, and use the wet brush to apply the gold leaf to each washer where you painted

● **JOANNA GOLLBERG**   **Approximate finished size:** 18 x 1³/₈ inches (45.7 x 3.5 cm)

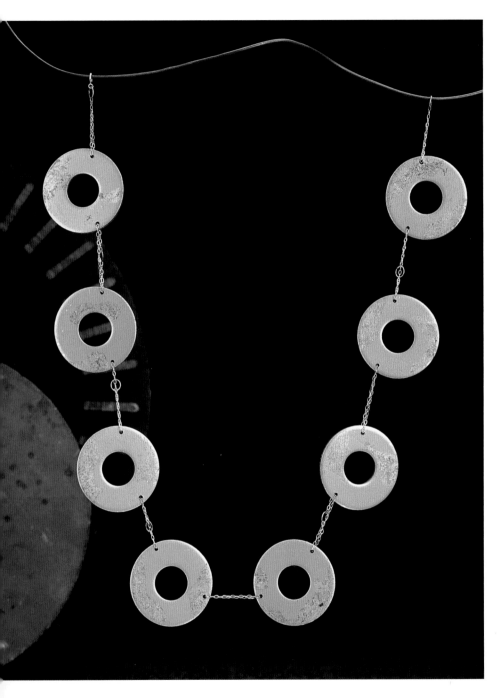

the fixative. Gently rub off any stray gold leaf with a soft cloth.

5. With the snips, cut nine sections of the gold-filled chain, each 2 inches (5 cm) long.

6. Thread one section through the right hole of one washer, and then through the left hole of the next washer.

7. Complete the chain by threading one of the 3 mm gold-filled jump rings through the ends of the chain. Open and close the jump ring by bending it back and forth with the flat-nose and chain-nose pliers. Never pull the ends apart. Connect all the washers in this manner. Then add a section of chain at one end of the necklace for the clasp.

8. Solder one jump ring together at a time, using 14k easy solder. Pickle and rinse, making sure the spray-painted washers stay out of the pickle.

9. Using the chain-nose and flat-nose pliers, attach the commercial spring clasp to the jump ring at one end of the necklace. The jump ring at the other end of the necklace will serve as the catch.

10. Rub each chain link with the brass brush to bring back its golden shine. Avoid brass brushing the washers, as this could damage the gold leaf or the paint finish.

CELL EARRINGS

The two earring sets shown on this page and the next give you some idea of the variations you can play with in making this piece. Wood makes a small but striking appearance here, in the form of the dark sawdust that colors the epoxy centers of the circles.

Tools

- Jeweler's saw and blades
- Sandpaper, 220- and 400-grit
- Wire cutters
- Round-nose pliers
- File
- Soldering set (see page 40)
- Third-hand tweezers
- Duct tape
- Disposable syringe, tiny spoon, or toothpick
- Flexible shaft with #61 drill bit
- Fast-drying epoxy
- Tweezers

Parts

- Assortment of sterling silver tubing: $1/8$, $1/4$, and $1/2$ inch (3, 6, and 13 mm) diameters
- Sterling silver wire, 16- or 19-gauge (depending on design)
- 2-part clear epoxy resin
- Sawdust or shavings of African Blackwood
- Fine silver wire, 20-gauge

● MOLLY DINGLEDINE   **Approximate finished size:** 1 x ½ inch (2.5 x 1.3 cm)

MOLLY DINGLEDINE   **Approximate finished size:** 1 x ½ inch (2.5 x 1.3 cm)

Assembly

1. Begin by designing a pair of earrings using the three different sizes of silver tubing. The larger earrings shown here, for example, each include two small, one medium, and one large circle. To help with the design, you can use a template of the various circle sizes to draw and cut out circles of paper to move around in different combinations.

2. Cut pieces of the silver tubing in your chosen combination about $1/8$ inch (3 mm) thick. Once you have all the pieces needed for your design, sand the rough edges with the sandpaper. Begin with 220 grit and then go to 400 grit to achieve a smooth edge.

3. If your design includes a thick wire to hang the circles from, as in the single-circle earrings shown on page 87, cut the 16-gauge wire to your desired length. (In those earrings, the straight wire is about $1/2$ inch, or 1.3 cm, long.) Then file or sand the ends to make them smooth.

4. If your design includes ear wires and not ear posts, bend the 19-gauge wire with round-nose pliers to make two ear wires. File or sand the ends of the wire to make them smooth.

5. On your soldering block, arrange the pieces of tubing according to your design; it may be easier to put flux on the pieces first, then arrange them and solder them together. If you are using a 16-gauge piece of wire in your design, solder the pieces of tubing together first. After cleaning the soldered piece in the pickle, apply more flux and solder the 16-gauge wire.

6. To solder the ear wire onto the piece, place the soldered tubing on the block upside down, and then place the ear wire in the third hand to hold it stable. Once all soldering is finished, clean up any solder with the sandpaper and make sure the pieces are dry before continuing.

7. Place a small piece of the duct tape on the back of any piece of tubing you want to fill with the resin. Make sure the tape adheres to the metal so resin does not seep out the bottom.

8. Mix the two-part clear epoxy resin according to its directions. Add the wood sawdust after you've completed the initial mixing (usually in about 2 minutes). Keep adding small amounts of sawdust as you mix until the epoxy resin turns the desired color and opacity.

9. Using the disposable syringe or tiny spoon (you can even use a toothpick), place the epoxy resin into the pockets of tubing until they fill up. Make sure the pieces don't move so the epoxy resin can set. If you notice air bubbles, gently blow on the piece until they surface, or you can put a fan on them. Be careful not to blow the unset resin out of the pockets!

10. After the resin has set, peel the duct tape from the back of the tubing. To set granules into the black epoxy, cut small pieces of 20-gauge fine silver wire to about $3/16$ to $1/4$ inch (5 to 6 mm) long. Ball up the ends to make tiny pins. Drill holes into the epoxy where you want the granules—be careful not to drill all the way through.

11. Mix up a small amount of fast-drying epoxy. Using the tweezers, put a tiny bit of epoxy on the end of the pin and stick it into the drilled hole. Let the epoxy set, then enjoy your new earrings.

FACT

African Blackwood (Dalbergia melanoxylon), also known as mpingo, is a small tree from sub-Saharan Africa. Its wood is prized for making many fine objects such as clarinets, bagpipes, and—with this project—earrings.

CITYSCAPE EARRINGS

The Union Jack perforated metal pattern we saw earlier in the Transom Brooch reappears here with a different result. In this project, you use a rolling mill to give a silver piece a texture that contrasts well with the strict shapes of the patterned triangles.

Tools

- Jeweler's saw and blades
- Torch
- Rolling mill
- Disk cutter
- Half-round file
- Scribe
- Steel ruler
- Center punch
- Flexible shaft
- Drill bit, 1.09 mm
- Soldering set (see page 40)
- Round-nose pliers
- Sandpaper, 400- to 1,000-grit
- Liver of sulfur

Parts

- Sterling silver sheet, 18-gauge
- Textured brass sheet, 16-gauge
- Perforated aluminum sheet metal, 28-gauge
- 2 jump rings, 16-gauge, 4 mm diameter
- Sterling silver wire, 22-gauge

Assembly

1. Cut a 4 x 2-inch (10.2 x 5 cm) piece of 18-gauge silver sheet. To anneal the metal, heat the piece with a torch until it turns a dull red color. Sandwich the silver between two pieces of brass, one of which is textured on one side. Place the sandwiched brass (with the textured side down on the silver) and silver pieces into a rolling mill, and roll them through the mill.

2. Anneal your texturized silver. Next, use a disk cutter to punch two ⁵/₈-inch (1.6 cm) circles out of the silver piece. Use a half-round file to file off the bottoms of both silver disks, filing off approximately 2 mm.

3. With the scribe and ruler, mark out two of the same shapes of perforated aluminum sheet metal you want to use. Following the scribe marks, saw out the shapes marked on the aluminum. Use a small half-round file to smooth the metal edges.

Approximate finished size: 2¹⁄₂ x ³⁄₄ x ¹⁄₁₆ inch (6.4 x 1.9 x 1.6 mm)

TONYA MOORE

4. Mark both the aluminum shapes 4 mm down from the slanted side with a scribe. Then mark both pieces 15 mm in from the 4 mm mark. Use a center punch to mark both 15 mm spots on the metal, and drill holes in each piece with the 1.09 mm drill bit in a flexible shaft.

5. Mark both textured silver pieces 5 mm across on the filed edge of the disk. This should be the center of the filed edge. Measure 2 mm up from the 5 mm mark, and dap with the center punch. Use the 1.09 mm drill bit to drill holes in both silver pieces. Next, measure 5 mm across on the rounded top edges of the disks, and mark with the scribe. Measure 2 mm down from the 5 mm mark, and dap with center punch. Drill holes in both disks with the same bit.

6. Place a 4 mm, 16-gauge jump ring through the hole in the texturized silver and perforated aluminum so that the perforated aluminum hangs below the textured silver with its slanted side out. Solder the jump rings with an easy solder. Make sure to only place the silver in pickle after soldering, as the aluminum will contaminate the pickle.

7. Cut two pieces of 22-gauge silver wire 3 inches (7.6 cm) long each. Ball up one end of each piece of wire using the torch. Place the wire through the hole on the top part of the silver disk, making sure the balled-up end is resting on the textured front of the earring. Pull the wire so it is sticking straight up from the earring. Approximately $1/3$ inch (8 mm) up from the hole, start rounding the wire with round-nose

pliers. (You can also use a 10 mm round mandrel to round the wire into an ear wire shape.) Sand the wire end with 400-grit sandpaper so that it won't prick your ear.

8. Finish the earrings by sanding them with 800-grit sandpaper. Paint the textured side of the sterling pieces with liver of sulfur to darken the recesses, then use 1,000-grit paper over the textured part to remove some of the patina.

TIP

In step 1, you can choose to sandwich a screen—or anything with a texture you find interesting—to transfer onto the silver between the two pieces of brass.

GALAXY NECKLACE

& SATELLITE BRACELET

You have a wide range of shapes and techniques to choose from in decorating the nine hanging necklace squares, and all nine bracelet squares. The designs created in this example look like they might even spell out something—at least in a different galaxy.

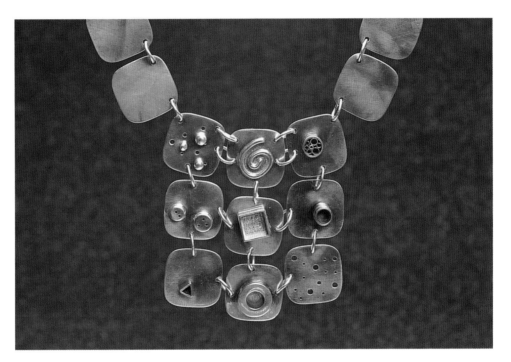

Tools

- **Fine-point permanent marker**
- **Flexible shaft**
- **Assorted drill bits**
- **Sandpaper, 400-grit, or kitchen scrubber pad**
- **Jeweler's saw and blades**
- **Tube-cutting jig**
- **Soldering set (see page 40)**
- **Wire cutters**
- **Round-nose pliers**
- **Polishing machine or other polishing equipment**

Parts

- **35 prepunched square metal shapes, 20 mm size**
- **5 crimp beads**
- **Casting grain (3 or 4 pieces)**
- **Tubing in various shapes and sizes**
- **Sterling silver round wire, 16g and 18g**
- **Jump rings, 18g and 7 mm diameter**
- **Silver sheet metal (approximately 22 gauge)**

Assembly

NECKLACE

1. Lay out 27 square pieces in the shape of the final necklace: nine pieces in a 3 x 3 square, nine squares in a line from the top left of those squares, and nine more leading from the top right square (see figure 1). Use a permanent marker to mark where the connecting holes will need to be drilled in each piece. Note: the two very top squares, which will be used to form the clasp, must have only one hole each.

2. With a flexible shaft and a very small drill bit (such as #70), make pilot holes at each spot marked in step 1, and then enlarge the holes with a #64 bit. Use fine sandpaper or a scrubbing pad to remove any burrs left from drilling.

3. For the nine squares that will be the necklace's focal point, you can choose from a variety of decorations and treatments. In different squares, you can:

- Drill holes of various sizes.
- Place five crimp beads in a random pattern on a fluxed square. Place tiny pieces of medium solder inside crimps, then heat the square from underneath until the solder flows.
- Place three pieces of presoldered round casting grain

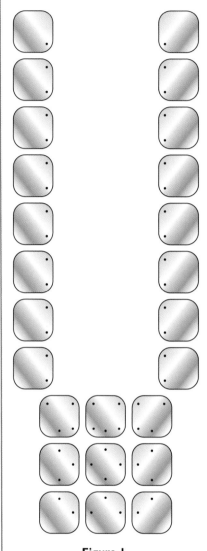

Figure 1

Arrange the metal shapes and mark drilling holes as shown.

on a fluxed square, and lightly solder from underneath.

- Cut one to five pieces of metal tubing approximately 3 mm long. (You can use tubing in a variety of shapes and diameters.) Lightly sand the top and bottom of each piece of tubing, then arrange them on a fluxed square with tiny pieces of medium solder inside the shapes. Heat underneath the square until the solder flows completely around the perimeter of the shapes.

4. To make the receiving end of the clasp: using the square piece that was placed at the end of the left side of the necklace (one of the two pieces with only one drilled hole), place the square so that the drilled hole is at the lower right corner. Drill a similar hole in the upper right corner, but with a larger drill bit (such as #58).

5. For the decorative dotted side of the clasp, place the other square with only one hole so that the hole is at the lower left. Drill random holes of various sizes through the square, but don't drill any holes near the top left corner. (That's where the clasp hook will go.) Remove any burrs with fine sandpaper or a scrubbing pad.

6. Use wire cutters to cut a piece of 16g silver wire approximately ¾

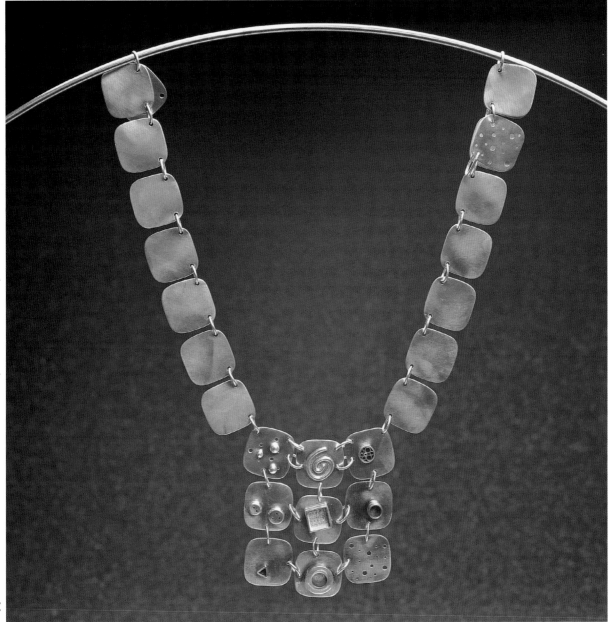

KRISTIN LORA

inch (1.9 cm) long. Use sandpaper or a scrubbing pad to sand the ends, making one end flat and the other rounded. Shape the wire with round-nose pliers to a curve that can serve as the necklace's clasp. Solder the flat end of the wire to the blank corner of the dotted square at the equivalent place as the hole in the other clasp square.

7. Now that all the squares have been prepared and decorated, it's time to assemble them in a necklace with the jump rings. Place all of the jump rings into the connecting holes, and lay the necklace on the soldering block upside down. (This way, the decorations will be facing the block and not get too close to the soldering flame.) Using tweezers, place each of the jump rings so the side with the opening is facing up. Place flux on each ring, and, using either a mini torch or a small tip, solder each ring closed with medium or easy solder. Then pickle the whole piece.

8. Polish the necklace. If you use a polishing machine, be sure to hold most of the necklace in your hands so that you won't catch the long ends in the machine. You can also polish using hand polishing tools and the flexible shaft. To achieve the brushed finished look, use wet/soapy very fine steel wool or a fine sanding sponge.

BRACELET

9. To make the bracelet, lay out nine metal squares in a line. Mark holes on the squares for the connecting jump rings (as in step 1), and drill and sand the holes (as in step 2). For the bracelet, the pattern of holes is as follows: the two squares at the ends (which will form the clasp) will have holes in two corners, while all other squares will have a hole in each of their four corners.

10. Decorate each square of the bracelet with one of the treatments described in step 3.

11. For the receiving end of the clasp, first cut a length of 18g sterling silver wire. Use round-nose pliers to form the wire into a C-shaped piece. Lightly hammer the two ends that will be attached to the square. Solder the two ends of the wire piece onto the edge at the end of one of the squares.

12. The other end of the clasp will be attached to the square at the opposite end of the bracelet. First, cut a piece of silver sheet $^5/_8$ x $^3/_8$ inches (16 x 10 mm). Hand form the piece to make it curve down at one narrower end, and curve slightly up at the other. Solder the down-curving end to the end of the square so that the clasp is on the back side of the bracelet.

13. To assemble the bracelet, put the nine squares in your desired order, with the clasp pieces at the ends, and attach with jump rings as in step 7. Then polish the bracelet, as described in step 8.

Approximate finished size: 7½ x ¾ inches (19 x 1.9 cm)

CLUSTER NECKLACE

The braided silver wire strips you purchase to begin this project are even more striking after you bend them into waves and oxidize their surfaces. A black cord and flared silver tubes complete the picture.

Tools

- Fine-point permanent marker or scribe
- Ruler
- Shears
- Sanding sticks, 220- and 400-grit
- Round-nose pliers
- Half-round pliers
- Safety goggles
- Latex gloves
- Brass brush
- Liquid dish soap
- Oxidizing solution
- Super fine steel wool (#0000)
- 2 pairs of chain-nose pliers
- Jeweler's saw and #3/0 saw blades
- Tube-cutting jig (optional)
- Flat file, #4 cut (optional)
- Steel block
- Dapping punch or tapered punch
- Chasing hammer
- Denatured alcohol
- Cotton swabs
- Cyanoacrylate glue

Parts

- 3 feet of sterling silver twisted wire strip (usually sold in 1-foot [30.5 cm] strips)
- 26 sterling silver jump rings, 20-gauge, 4 mm ID
- 2 ear wires
- 50 mm sterling silver medium wall tubing, 3 mm ID
- 7 mm sterling silver medium wall tubing, 5 mm ID
- 1 sterling silver jump ring, 16-gauge, 6.5 mm inside diameter (ID)
- 46 cm rubber cord, 3 mm diameter
- Sterling silver end caps with clasp, 3 mm ID

Approximate finished size: 6 x 8 x $^3/_{16}$ inches (15.2 x 20.3 cm x 5 mm)

Assembly

1. To create the necklace and earrings, you will need the following lengths of twisted wire strip:

- 1 piece each of 1½, 2, and 2¼ inches (3.8, 5, and 5.7 cm)
- 3 pieces each of 1¾, 2½, and 3 inches (4.4, 6.4, and 7.6 cm)

2. To create a finished end from which to start, use a permanent marker or scribe to mark a curved line on one end of a 1-foot (30.5 cm) length of wire strip at the point where the twisted wires intersect. Be sure your line follows the curve of the wire pattern.

3. Using a ruler, measure the desired strip length from the scribed line you made in the previous step. Just beyond the desired measurement, find the point in the pattern where the wires cross. Mark the wire just to the outside of this intersection. Your line should follow the pattern, but curve in the opposite direction of the line in step 2. Next, scribe a line curving in the same direction as the one in step 2, just to the inside of the immediately adjacent intersecting point in the pattern. The wire between the two lines you just scribed will be scrap that will not be used.

4. Repeat steps 2 and 3 on each foot-long strip to mark the 12 lengths of wire needed for this project. Then use shears to cut the wire on each scribed line.

5. Remove any burs, and smooth the ends of each section of wire with a 220-grit sanding stick, using a curved stroke to follow the shape of the pattern. Continue to smooth and round the ends with a 400-grit sanding stick.

6. Each of the earrings will be made from the following three lengths of wire: 3, 2½, and 1¾ inches (7.6, 6.4, and 4.4 cm). Mark two of each of these lengths for later identification. The necklace will be made from the remaining six pieces.

7. Make a loop on one end of each wire. To ensure that the loops are identical, use a permanent marker to mark the jaws of the round-nose pliers where the jaw diameter is approximately 3.5 mm. Holding the end of the wire at the mark on the jaws, with 2 mm protruding, use your fingers to bend the wire around the pliers to form the loop. Repeat with each section of wire.

8. Hold a section of wire with half-round pliers below the loop formed in the previous step. Grip the wire with the rounded jaw of the pliers on the side opposite the opening of the loop. Bend the wire over the half-round jaw of the pliers. Flip the pliers over and bend a curve just next to the previous curve, but in the opposite direction, to create a wave in the wire. Continue making alternate curves along the length of the wire, flipping the pliers each time, until the wave pattern reaches the end. Repeat on each wire.

9. Oxidize the wire components before assembly. Begin by putting on safety goggles and latex gloves and thoroughly cleaning the pieces with a brass brush and soapy water. Dip the pieces in the oxidizing solution until they turn black. Rinse them thoroughly and dry.

10. Remove the oxide from the surface of the wires with super fine steel wool. The recessed areas will remain black, emphasizing the design of the twisted wire.

11. To begin assembly, close 12 jump rings, using two pairs of chain-nose pliers, and set aside. Then open the remaining 14 jump rings.

12. Feed an open jump ring through a closed jump ring and the loop of a wavy wire section from step 8, and close it to create a dangle. Repeat for each wavy wire. You will have two open jump rings remaining.

13. Make each earring with three dangles from step 12. Placing the longest dangle in the center, feed one of the remaining open jump rings through the top jump ring of these dangles and the loop of an ear wire. Be sure the openings on the wavy wire loops face the back of the earring. Close the jump ring. Repeat this process to create the second earring.

Approximate finished size: 1½ x 3 x 1 inch (3.8 x 7.6 x 2.5 cm)

14. To make the necklace, start by annealing the pieces of tubing. Using a jeweler's saw with a #3/0 blade, cut the 50 mm length of tubing into 10 pieces, 5 mm long each. A tube-cutting jig makes this job simple.

15. Remove any burrs and smooth the ends of each piece of tubing, including the 7 mm diameter piece, with a file (if necessary) and sanding sticks.

16. Set the pieces of tubing upright on a steel block. Place a dapping punch or tapered punch in the end of the first piece of tubing. Holding the punch vertical and parallel to the tubing walls, strike it with a chasing hammer until the tubing starts to flare out at the end. Flip the piece of tubing over, and start to flare the other end. Continue to flip the piece, flaring the ends until they are identical. Repeat on each piece of tubing.

17. Open the 16-gauge jump ring, and feed it through the largest piece of flared tubing and the top jump rings on the six remaining wire and jump ring dangles. Be sure the openings on the wavy wire loops all face the same direction. Close the jump ring.

18. String five pieces of the smaller tubing onto the rubber cord. Feed the cord through the larger piece of tubing with the wires hanging down. String the remaining five pieces of smaller tubing on the opposite side of the dangle. The smaller sections of tubing should stay in place. If they slide freely, flare them more with the punch until the middle of the tubing compresses to the correct inside diameter.

19. Remove any oxides from the inside of the end caps with a small piece of sandpaper. Clean the inside of the end caps and the ends of the rubber cord with denatured alcohol on a cotton swab. Allow pieces to dry.

20. Apply a very small amount of cyanoacrylate glue to one end of the cord and the inside of one end cap. (A piece of broken saw blade works well for this.) Insert the cord into the end cap, and hold firmly in place for 30 seconds. Repeat with the other end cap. Allow the pieces to dry for at least 10 minutes before testing the bond.

21. To finish the necklace and earring set, add a satin luster by burnishing lightly with a brass brush and soapy water.

CITY LIGHTS STICK PIN

The sparkly fireworks of this piece are meant to evoke the rhythm that drives a crowded city. And, as often happens in a big city, you'll find an unusual juxtaposition of elements here—tubes and wires, jewelry crown settings, and guitar strings.

Tools

- Riveting hammer
- Wire snips
- Soldering set (see page 40)
- Third-arm tweezers
- Steel ruler
- Round needle file
- Jeweler's saw and blades
- Radial emery discs
- Hammer handpiece
- Diamond tip
- Flexible shaft
- Epoxy kit
- Steel block

Parts

- 9 silver crown set findings: three each of 2.6 mm, 2.9 mm, and 3.7 mm
- Brass round wire: 1.6 mm, 2.2 mm, and 2.6 mm
- Sterling silver round wire, 1 mm and 2 mm
- Sterling silver tubing: 1 mm, 1.5 mm, 2.5 mm, and 3 mm
- 3 guitar strings, 36-gauge nickel-wound electric
- Silver rod
- Plastic tube

Assembly

1. Place the crown sets upside down, and hammer them down until the four prongs on the crown are bent outwards.

2. Search for the suitable size of brass wire that can feed through the different crown sets, then use snips to cut the appropriate wires into a ½-inch-long (1.3 cm) piece for each set; you will have nine wires in all.

3. Ball up one end on each of the wires with a torch. Feed the other end of each wire through the matching crown set. Position them on the third arm with the wire and sets upside-down, and solder them together.

4. Cut nine pieces of the 1 mm sterling silver wire: six about 1 inch (2.5 cm) long, and three about ½ inch (1.3 cm) long. File the ends of the wire pieces round with a round needle file.

5. Solder one of the nine wire pieces onto the side of each of the crown sets. After soldering, cut away the excess part of the brass wire with a jeweler's saw and a file.

Approximate finished size: 7 x 2 x ½ inch (17.8 x 5 x 1.3 cm)

● **VICTORIA CHO**

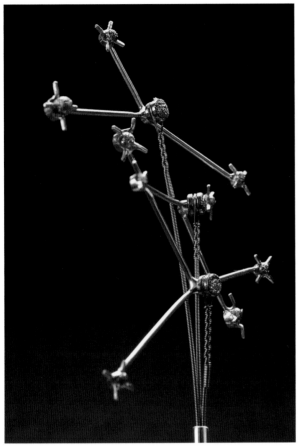

A side view shows how the guitar strings are looped around brass caps that are attached to the three "sparkle" assemblies.

6. Cut three ½-inch (1.3 cm) lengths of the 1.5 mm sterling silver tubing. These will form the main body of each of the three sparkles. On your soldering block, position two long and one short piece of the wires soldered in step 5 around each of the three pieces of tubing. (See the photo of the piece here for an idea of what angles to position the pieces from the center.) Solder the ends of the wires to the sides of the tubing pieces.

7. Cut three guitar strings at these lengths from the end of the string with a round brass cap: 1½, 2, and 2½ inches (3.8, 5, and 6.4 cm). Position the string onto the center of the top side of the three tubing pieces from step 6, and solder together.

8. After it is soldered, use a hammer handpiece with a flat tip to rivet down the excess part on the tubing onto the rim of the brass ring on the guitar string wire. Give the end of the tube a tap with the riveting hammer for tightening and holding the piece together.

9. With a diamond tip on the hammer handpiece, create sparkling texture on the top surface of the brass circles, as well as on each of the balled-up brass wires on the crown sets.

10. Cut a 1½-inch (3.8 cm) piece of 3 mm tubing. Cut a 3-inch (7.6 cm) piece of 2 mm wire, and thread 2 mm of it into the end of the 3 mm tubing, soldering them together. Sharpen the other end of the wire to a pin point with a file.

11. For the stud of the stick pin, cut a ³/₈-inch (9.5 mm) piece of the 2.5 mm tube, and close one end of the tube by soldering sterling silver scrap onto it. File and round both ends of the tube. Epoxy a plastic wire (or rubber cord) into the tubing stud. The open end should fit snugly over the pin point.

12. To finish assembly, thread the guitar-string ends of the three sparkle sets into the open end of the 3 mm sterling silver tube from step 10, using epoxy to keep them in place.

SECRET TREASURE

EARRINGS

Jump rings usually find themselves in supporting roles in jewelry construction, but here they are the stars of the show. Tiny golden balls within the earrings make cameo appearances as the barely seen (and sometimes faintly heard) hidden treasure.

Approximate finished size: $3/8$ x $3/8$ x $3/4$ inch (9.5 x 9.5 mm x 1.9 cm)

● MICHELLE CHAN

Tools

- **Drawing template**
- **Fine-point permanent marker**
- **Scrap of copper or brass sheet metal**
- **Jeweler's saw and blades**
- **File**
- **Soldering set (see page 40)**
- **Brass brush**
- **Scribe**
- **Flexible shaft with ball burr attachment**
- **Polishing machine with pink buffing wheel**
- **Polishing compound**

Parts

- **24 sterling silver jump rings, 5 mm diameter**
- **2 silver earring posts**
- **22-gauge sterling silver sheet metal**
- **Scrap pieces of gold**
- **2 earring post clasps**

Assembly

1. With a circle template and a permanent marker, trace out a semicircle ³/₈ inch (9.5 mm) in diameter onto a piece of copper or brass sheet metal. Trace out a handle on the flat side of the semicircle. Cut out this shape with a jeweler's saw, and file the edges smooth.

2. Hold the cutout semicircle by the handle, and use it to carve into the soldering brick and make a dome shape.

3. Place six jump rings into the carved dome, with one centered on the bottom of the dome and the other five arranged around its sides, as shown in figure 1. Apply flux to each soldering joint, and solder with medium solder. Quench the piece in water, put it in a pickle solution, and after a few minutes take it out and clean it with a brass brush. Repeat this step three more times to create the four halves that will be combined into two earrings.

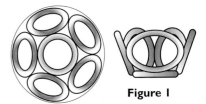

Figure I

This top view and side view shows the arrangement of five jump rings around the one at the bottom of the carved-out dome.

4. With a scribe and a circle template, trace out two 5 mm circles (the same size as the jump rings you are using) onto a piece of silver sheet metal. Solder an earring post onto the center of the circle for each. Quench, pickle, and clean.

5. To make small metal balls for inside the hollow earrings (the "secret treasure"), first use a ball burr the same size as the ball you would like—2 mm works well—to carve a hole into your soldering brick. Melt scrap pieces of gold into the carved shape; then quench, pickle, and clean. Make either one or two balls for each earring.

6. Cut out the two circles with earring posts from step 4 with a jeweler's saw, and file the edges smooth. Thread the earring post through a jump ring from the inside of the dome, then apply flux, and solder the circle to the jump ring with easy solder. Quench, pickle, and clean.

7. Take one of the jump ring domes that has an earring post, and match it to one of the domes without a post. Put the two halves of the earring together, enclosing one or two of the small gold balls you made in step 5 within the two halves. Apply flux to all soldering joints, and solder with easy solder. Quench, pickle, and clean. Do the same with the other two domes.

8. Finish up the two earrings with a pink wheel, and polish them with a buffing wheel using polishing compound. Insert commercial clasps into the earring posts.

BUBBLES RING

Yes, even plumbing parts can be transformed into stunning design elements. You use the middle section of a copper pipe coupling to create the primary decorative and structural element of this cocktail ring.

Tools

- Half-round file, 2-cut
- Sanding sticks and sandpaper, 220- and 400-grit
- Scribe or permanent marker
- Dividers
- Safety goggles
- Jeweler's saw with #2/0 and #3/0 blades
- ¾-inch (1.9 cm) wooden dowel
- Graph paper

- Center punch
- Flexible shaft
- Drill bit, 1.2 mm
- Sanding drums, 220- and 400-grit
- Caliper
- Tubing cutter
- Soldering set (see page 40)
- Solder shears
- Barrette needle file, 4-cut

- Circle template
- Ring mandrel
- Ball peen or cross peen hammer
- Mallet
- Steel block
- Abrasive pad (optional)
- Super fine (#0000) steel wool (optional)
- Polishing buffs, wheels, and compounds (optional)

Parts

- Copper pipe coupling (adapter), diameter of ¾ inch to ½ inch (1.9 to 1.3 cm) (available from hardware or plumbing-supply store)
- Sterling silver tubing, 6.1 mm inside diameter (ID), 4.8 mm ID, 5.1 mm ID, 4 mm ID, 2.3 mm ID
- 1-inch (2.5 cm) length of sterling silver round wire, 16-gauge
- 2-inch (5 cm) length of sterling silver low-dome, half-round wire, 6 x 2 mm
- Hard silver solder

Approximate finished size: 1 x 1 x 1 1/8 inches (2.5 x 2.5 x 2.9 cm); ring size 7.5

● **CHRISTINE DHEIN**

Assembly

1. File off the raised part number from the outside of the coupling with the flat side of a half-round file. Smooth the area with sanding sticks. Then file both ends of the coupling flat, perpendicular to the walls.

2. Scribe two lines around the circumference of the coupling with the divider; one that is 15 mm from the top, and the other 11 mm from the bottom. For this project, the end of the coupling with the ¾-inch (1.9 cm) diameter is the top and the ½-inch (1.3 cm) end is the bottom. The center section, between the two scribed lines, is the part that will be used (see figure 1).

13 mm

Figure 1

The middle section of the coupling, 13 mm high, becomes the ring's basic element.

3. Wearing safety goggles, slice through the coupling using a jeweler's saw and a #2 blade, cutting just to the outside of the scribed lines. You can insert a ¾-inch (1.9 cm) wooden dowel into the top end of the coupling to help stabilize the piece during sawing.

4. File both ends of the center section back to the scribed lines with a flat file.

5. Center the bottom of the coupling on a piece of graph paper, and scribe lines on the vertical and horizontal axes to indicate the centerlines. Then use the divider to measure 2.5 mm from the bottom of the coupling, and make a mark at the four points where the centerlines and dividers meet.

6. Create a divot at each mark with a center punch. Drill a hole at two opposing divots with a flexible shaft and 1.2 mm bit. Check that a 16-gauge wire fits tightly in each hole, and remove the wire.

7. With a sanding drum in the flexible shaft, remove the burs and smooth the interior surface of the small end of the coupling. Then use 220- and 400-grit sanding sticks to remove the burs and smooth the exterior surfaces.

8. Use the depth gauge on a caliper to measure the depth of the bottom half of the coupling; this will be approximately 6 mm. Cut the following pieces of silver tubing to the length measured in the pre-vious step using a tubing cutter and jeweler's saw with a #3/0 blade:

- **2 pieces: 4 mm ID**
- **2 pieces: 2.3 mm ID**
- **1 piece each: all remaining sizes**

9. Remove the burs and smooth the ends of each piece of tubing with a 400-grit sanding stick. Clean the outside of each piece with the sanding stick or an abrasive pad.

10. Insert the pieces of tubing into the small opening in the coupling. Use a pattern similar to that visible in the photo below. The fit should be tight enough to hold the pieces in place. If necessary, remove metal evenly from the inside of the coupling with the sanding drum until the final piece of tubing can be pressed into position. Position the top of each piece of silver tubing flush with the flat section on the inside of the coupling.

The varied slices of silver tubing are packed tightly within the narrower end of the copper coupling.

13. Put the assembly on the charcoal block, with the large end facing downward, and flux each joint to be soldered, including the joints of the riveting wires. Lift the piece and touch each joint to be soldered from underneath with a damp flux brush. This will pull the flux through each seam. Then place the disk cut from the soldering pad on the charcoal block. Press the large end of the coupling onto the disk until it supports the silver tubing.

14. Cut pallions of silver solder with the shears, and place one on each joint with a damp flux brush or tweezer. Solder with a large, bushy flame. Concentrate the heat on the copper piece. Avoid heating the riveting wires directly. The wires must be soldered at a 90° angle to the coupling wall. Remove any excess solder from the wires and their solder joints with a barrette needle file. Smooth with a 400-grit sanding stick.

15. To shape the bottom of the coupling to match the shape of a finger, place the centering mark from a 3/4-inch (1.9 cm) circle template at the remaining divots from step 6, and scribe an arc with the divot at the top of the arc (see figure 2 again). Carve away the metal below the arcs by filing across the bottom of the coupling with a half-round file. Then smooth this filed area with sandpaper wrapped around a 3/4-inch (1.9 cm) dowel. The top of the arcs should rest comfortably on your finger.

11. Cut 2 pieces of 16-gauge round wire, approximately 12 mm in length, remove any burs, and insert in each of the holes from step 6. These wires will be used to rivet the top of the ring to the shank. Position the wires flush with the inside of the coupling. They will protrude approximately 10 mm and be perpendicular to the outside walls (see figure 2).

Figure 2

The two protruding silver wires will later become rivets to attach the ring band, and the arc scribed here will be cut to fit the bottom of ring to the top of your finger.

12. To make cleanup easy, the tubing will be soldered in place with the large end of the coupling facing downward. Create a prop to hold the tubing in place during soldering by putting the discarded piece of ¾-inch (1.9 cm) copper piping from step 3 on a broken piece of white soldering pad. Scribe a circle on the soldering pad by tracing around the inside of the copper pipe. Cut a disk out of the soldering pad with a jeweler's saw and #3/0 blade. Check the fit, and file if necessary to create a disk that can be inserted into the pipe. Smooth the top and bottom surfaces of the disk by rubbing in a "figure 8" motion on sandpaper or smooth cement. Be sure the top and bottom edges are parallel.

16. To make the ring shank, cut a 2-inch (5 cm) piece of low dome wire, and anneal. File both ends of the wire flat.

17. To lay out the location for the holes that will accept the riveting wires, use the dividers to lightly scribe two lines across the curved surface of the wire that are 2.5 mm from each end. Then set the divider to 3.3 mm, and place one leg along the length of the wire near the end. Use the other leg of the divider to scribe short lines at each end of the wire that are perpendicular to the lines from the previous step, and divide the width of the wire in half.

18. Use a center punch to make a deep divot at the intersection of the lines from the previous step. Drill a hole in the wire at each divot with a 1.2 mm drill bit, and remove any burs.

19. Round the corners on the ends of the wire with the flat side of the half-round file. Smooth with 220- and 400-grit sanding sticks.

20. Place the center of the wire on a ring mandrel, flat side down, at size 6. Bend the wire into a "U" shape by hammering on either side of the center section until the opening in the "U" is slightly wider than the small end of the coupling. The legs of the "U" must remain straight and parallel. Do not hammer the legs against the mandrel.

21. Insert one of the rivet wires into a hole on the inside of the ring shank with the large end of the coupling facing away from the shank. Press the ring shank flush against the coupling. With your fingers, pry the legs of the "U" open to insert the other wire into the hole on the opposite side of the shank. The first wire must remain in position.

22. Close the opening in the shank by placing one leg of the shank on a wooden surface, with the coupling and the rivet wire hanging over the edge. Use a mallet to hammer above the curve in the shank until both legs touch the coupling.

23. File the ends of the rivets flat with the barrette needle file until each wire protrudes 0.6 mm from the ring shank. This metal will become a rivet head.

24. Place one leg of the shank parallel to the top of a steel block so only the riveting wire touches the steel. The coupling should hang over the edge of the block. Use a ball peen or cross peen hammer to strike several blows to the end of the exposed rivet wire. Flip the piece over and repeat this step.

25. Continue flipping the piece and hammering evenly to create symmetrical rivet heads until they hold the pieces in place securely. Be careful not to hammer the shank surrounding the rivet head.

26. Smooth and shape the head of the rivet with a barrette needle file and a 400-grit sanding stick. Be sure the edges of the rivet head are flush with the shank.

27. Apply the desired finish to the ring. The ring pictured was finished with super fine steel wool on the outside surfaces and a high polish on the inside of the coupling.

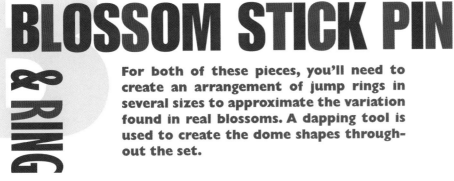

● **MEDIUM**

BLOSSOM STICK PIN & RING

For both of these pieces, you'll need to create an arrangement of jump rings in several sizes to approximate the variation found in real blossoms. A dapping tool is used to create the dome shapes throughout the set.

Tools

- Drawing template
- Scribe
- Jeweler's saw and blades
- File
- Soldering set (see page 40)
- Brass brush
- Dapping block
- Rubber mallet
- Dapping punch
- Snips
- Tweezers
- Flexible shaft
- 5 mm ball bur attachment
- Center punch
- Fine-point permanent marker
- Third arm tweezers
- Drill bit, 1 mm
- Emery bit, 120-, 400-, and 600-grit
- Buffing wheel
- Polishing compound
- Ring mandrel

Parts

- Sterling silver sheet metal, 20-gauge
- Small scraps of gold
- Sterling silver round wire, 1 mm
- Sterling silver jump rings in various sizes from 4 mm to 6 mm diameter
- Sterling silver tubing, 2 mm
- Rubber cord, 1.5 mm size
- Sterling silver round wire, 3.5 mm

Assembly

STICK PIN

1. Use a circle template and a scribe to trace a 1-inch (2.5 cm) circle onto a piece of sterling silver sheet metal. Cut out the circle with a jeweler's saw, and file its edges smooth.

2. With a small torch, anneal the circle until it turns bright red, quench in water, and then place the piece into a pickle solution. Take out the piece after a few minutes, and clean it with a brass brush.

3. Place the circle piece into the circle dapping block. Form it into a dome shape with a rubber mallet and the matching dapping punch.

4. Use snips to cut six pieces of 1 mm wire, with each at least ³/₈ inch (9.5 mm) in length. To ball up the ends of the wires, hold one with tweezers and point the end of your torch's flame to the tip of the wire until it

113

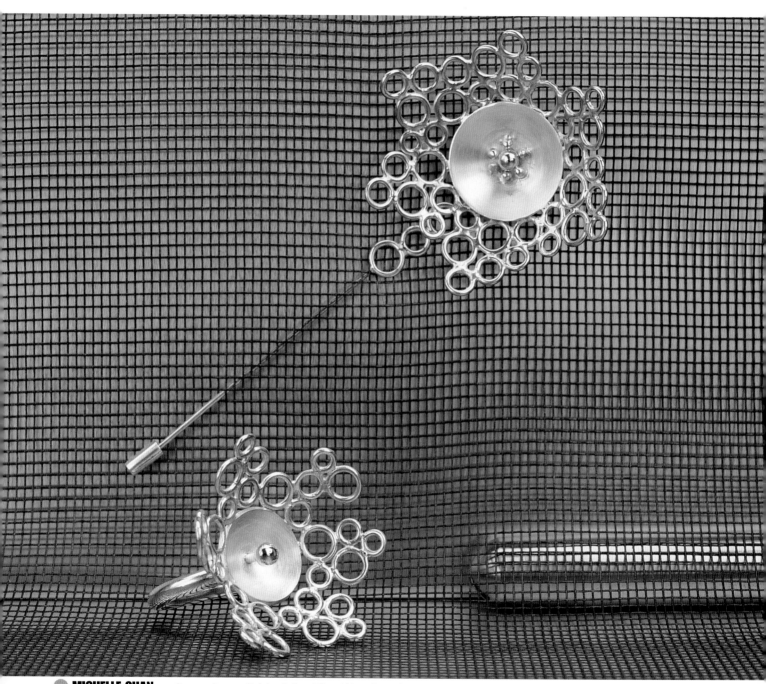

● **MICHELLE CHAN**   **Approximate finished size: Ring** 1³/₈ x 1³/₈ x 1³/₈ inches (3.5 x 3.5 x 3.5 cm); **Pin** 1³/₄ x 1³/₄ x 4 inches (4.4 x 4.4 x 10.2 cm)

114

begins to ball up. (Safety note: Make sure that you keep the hand that is holding the tweezers up high, as much above the flame as possible.) Remove the flame when the balled-up end is the desired size. Repeat the step with the other four wires. When you are done with each wire, quench it in water and put it in the pickle. After a few minutes in the pickle, clean each piece with a brass brush.

5. To make the gold ball for the center of the piece, first drill a hole into your soldering brick with a 5 mm ball bur. Melt some scraps of gold into the hole to form a ball. Cut a piece of 1 mm silver wire $5/8$ inch (1.6 cm) in length. Apply flux to the surfaces of the gold ball and the wire, and solder the tip of the wire onto the surface of the ball using hard solder. Quench, pickle, and clean.

A closer view of the center of the stick pin shows where you position the five silver balled-up wires around one wire topped with a golden ball.

6. With a center punch, mark one spot at the center of the domed disk (the inside part) and five spots in a circle around it for drilling holes to thread the balled wires. Use a 1 mm drill bit to drill the holes. Thread the wires into the holes, with the wire you soldered a ball

to in the center. Turn the piece upside down, apply flux to each soldering point, and solder with medium solder. Be careful not to melt the wire in the center. Quench, pickle, and clean.

7. Trim the excess wires sticking out from the back of the dome except for the one in the middle. File the surface of these outside wires smooth.

8. Cut a piece of 1 mm wire 2 inches (5 cm) in length. Put the wire into the flexible shaft, and use emery paper to taper one end of it. Stop when a pin point is formed.

9. Clamp the dome by the wire in the middle. Line up three jump rings and the pin point wire, and apply flux to each soldering point. Solder the pieces together; then quench, pickle, and clean.

10. Using the circle template, pick a circle one size bigger than the size that you used for your dome, and cut it out and prepare it according to the instructions in steps 1 and 2. Trace out the circle with a permanent marker onto your soldering brick. Place jump rings in various sizes along the outside edge of the circle, mapping out your design as you go. Apply flux to all soldering joints, and solder with medium solder. Quench, pickle, and clean.

11. Place the jump ring assembly into the dapping block, and gently use a mallet and dapping tool to give it a slight dome form. Using a third arm for support, solder the jump ring piece onto the edge of the dome with easy solder. Quench, pickle, and clean.

12. To make a stick pin back, cut a piece of 2 mm tubing $1/4$ inch (6 mm) in length, then solder the tubing onto a piece of 20-gauge silver sheet metal. Cut the piece out from the sheet metal, and file smooth the rough edges. Insert 1.5 mm rubber cord into the tubing, and drill a hole into the center with a 1 mm drill bit.

13. Clean your piece with emery paper, starting from 120 grit and working your way down to 600 grit. Finish with a buffing wheel, and polish your piece with polishing compound.

RING

14. To make a circle piece for the center of the ring, follow the instructions in steps 1 through 3 above, only use a ¾ inch (1.9 cm) circle instead of the 1 inch (2.5 cm) circle used for the stick pin.

15. As in step 5 above, drill a hole into your soldering brick with a 5 mm ball bur, melt some scrap gold to form a ball, and then solder the ball to a ⅝ inch (1.6 cm) piece of 1 mm silver wire.

16. Mark the center of the dome with a center punch, and drill a hole with a 1 mm drill bit.

17. Thread the balled wire into the hole with .5 mm of the wire sticking out from the back. Apply flux and solder the joint. Quench, pickle, and clean.

18. To calculate the length of silver wire needed to make your ring band, follow this formula: (inside diameter + metal thickness) x 3.14. Use a caliper to measure the inside diameter of your ring size from a ring sizer. Plug that number into the formula, along with 3.5 mm for the thickness of the silver wire you will use here, and calculate the required length. Cut a piece of wire to that length.

19. Anneal the wire, quench it in water, and form your ring band with a ring mandrel. Form until the two ends of the wire meet. Apply flux to the joint, and solder. Quench, pickle, and clean. Put the ring back onto the ring mandrel, and hammer it around to make sure the band is round. Take the ring off the mandrel, and cut open the seam with a jeweler's saw. Bend the two ends away from each other to create a spiral shape. File smooth the edges.

20. With a center punch, mark out a spot near one of the ends of the ring band where you will insert the center wire from your dome. Drill this hole with a 1 mm drill bit. Insert the dome's wire into the ring band, apply flux onto the joint, and solder with medium solder. Quench, pickle, and clean. If any excess wire sticks out from the ring band, trim it. File any edges smooth.

21. Similarly to step 10 above, trace a circle one size bigger than the size that you used for your dome onto your soldering brick, and create and solder a design of jump rings around it. Then, as in step 11, give the jump ring assembly a slight dome shape in a dapping block, and solder it to the edge of the ring's dome.

22. Finish your ring as you did the stick pin in step 13: with emery paper, a buffing wheel, and polishing compound.

GALLERY

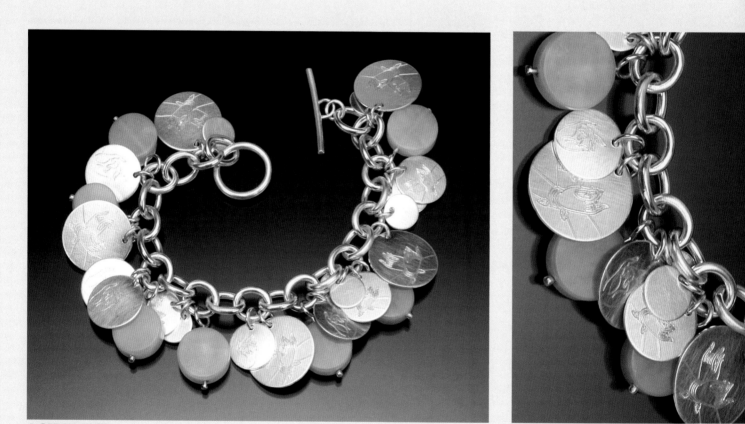

● SARAH HOOD
Jade Mudra Bracelet, 2006
2.5 x 18.5 x 0.5 cm
Sterling silver discs and cable chain, coin-cut jade;
engraved, soldered, hand finished
Photos by Doug Yaple

JENNY WINDLER
Collecting Dust, 2005
2.5 x 1.9 x 1.9 cm
Sterling silver, sterling silver dust, stainless
steel washers and machine screws, glass;
hand cut, formed, assembled, soldered
Photo by artist

2 ROSES
Hi-Tek Radaii, 2006
48 x 48 x 1.3 cm
Circuit board components, sterling silver tube;
hand fabricated, cold connected
Photo by Corliss Rose

● SIM LUTTIN
800 Wishes Home, 2006
25 x 10 cm
Fine silver, nylon and steel cord;
hand fabricated, forged
Photo by Kevin O'Mooney

● SO YOUNG PARK
Nativity II, 2004
5 x 10 x 5 cm
Sterling silver, pearls; hammered, soldered
Photo by Ga Rim Hong

● SADIE WANG
Untitled, 2004
1.3 x 45.7 x 0.3 cm
Sterling silver, 14-karat gold, resin;
hand fabricated
Photo by Azad Photo

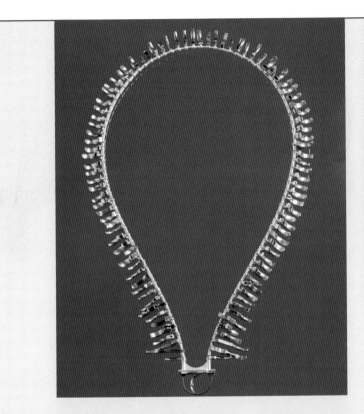

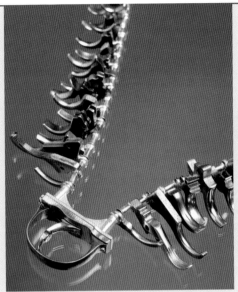

● **BORIS BALLY**
Brave 2, 2006
62.5 x 30.5 x 3 cm
Steel handgun triggers, cast 14-karat
yellow gold, white sapphire, sterling silver;
fabricated, tube set
Photos by Aaron Usher III

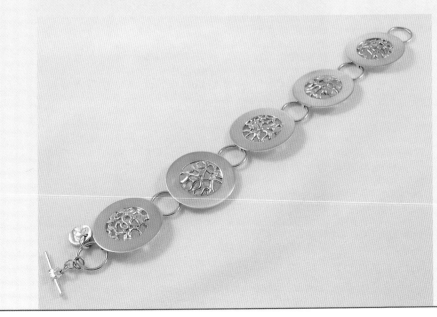

● **DEBORAH MARIE FEHRENBACH**
Sea Lace Bracelet, 2007
18.5 x 2.5 x 0.5 cm
Sterling silver washers, cast insets,
tubing, jump rings, and wire; lost
wax cast inset, hand fabricated
Photo by artist

JOANNA GOLLBERG
Ladder Choker, 2002
8.5 x 4.5 x 0.3 cm
Sterling silver wire, pearls; hand cut, riveted
Photo by keithwright.com

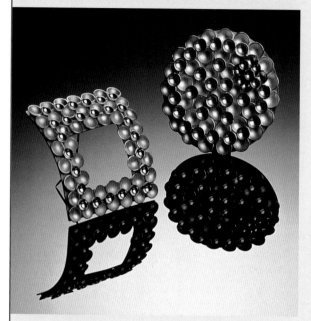

SO YOUNG PARK
Nativity Series Brooch, 2005
5 x 5 x 0.5 cm
18-karat yellow gold, sterling silver; hammered,
soldered
Photo by Ga Rim Hong

JOANNA GOLLBERG
Polka-Dot Tube Earrings, 2002
3 x 1.5 x 0.3 cm
Sterling silver tubing and wire, pearls; hand cut,
cold connected
Photo by keithwright.com

CHARTS

The Brown and Sharp (B. & S.) Gauge for Sheet Metal

GAUGE NUMBER	THICKNESS IN INCHES	THICKNESS IN MILLIMETERS
3/0	.409	10.388
2/0	.364	9.24
1/0	.324	8.23
1	.289	7.338
2	.257	6.527
3	.229	5.808
4	.204	5.18
5	.181	4.59
6	.162	4.11
7	.144	3.66
8	.128	3.24
9	.114	2.89
10	.101	2.565
11	.090	2.28
12	.080	2.03
13	.071	1.79
14	.064	1.625
15	.057	1.447
16	.050	1.27
17	.045	1.114
18	.040	1.016
19	.035	.889
20	.031	.787
21	.028	.711
22	.025	.635
23	.022	.558
24	.020	.508
25	.017	.431
26	.015	.381
27	.014	.376
28	.012	.304
29	.011	.29
30	.01	.254
31	.008	.203
32	.0079	.199
33	.007	.177
34	.006	.152
35	.0055	.142
36	.005	.127

Annealing Temperatures for Metal

METAL	FAHRENHEIT	CELSIUS
Copper	700°–1200°	370°–650°
Brass	800°–1380°	430°–750°
Silver	1120°–1300°	600°–700°
Gold *	1200°–1380°	650°–750°

*other than fine gold

Melting Temperatures for Metal

METAL	FAHRENHEIT	CELSIUS
Aluminum	1220°	660°
Gold*	1600°–1830°	880°–1000°
Silver	1640°	890°
Brass	1660°	900°
Bronze	1945°	1060°
Copper	1980°	1080°
Nickel silver	2020°	1110°
Stainless steel	2500°	1371°
Low-carbon steel	2750°	1511°
Iron	2793°	1535°

*other than fine gold

Solder Flow Points

SOLDER TYPE	FAHRENHEIT	CELSIUS
Easy	1325°	711°
Medium	1390°	747°
Hard	1425°	773°
Eutectic	1460°	793°
IT	1490°	809°

CONTRIBUTING ARTISTS

ELISA BONGFELDT maintains a studio in Berkeley, California, where she makes one-of-a-kind and production jewelry. A graduate of the California College of Arts and Crafts (now California College of the Arts), she exhibits her work internationally.

MICHELLE CHAN is a recent graduate of the Jewelry program at the Ontario College of Art and Design. Inspired by everyday objects, she seeks in her jewelry making to execute series of pieces that present her conceptual ideas with integrity and passion. She also hopes through her work to help promote Canadian artistry.

VICTORIA CHO first began working with metal in 2002 at the Ontario College of Art and Design in their jewelry and metalsmithing design program. Her textured and inventive objects are inspired by her sense of rhythm, energy, enthusiasm, and fun. Cho has shown her work in exhibitions and competitions around Toronto, Canada, and in her hometown of Hong Kong.

CHRISTINE DHEIN is an educator, writer, and award-winning designer who lives in San Francisco, California. She is the assistant director of San Francisco's Revere Academy of Jewelry Arts, where she teaches keum-boo and fabrication. Dhein has published articles on topics such as tool tips and keum-boo, and her jewelry has been featured in a number of books such as *The Art and Craft of Making Jewelry* and *500 Earrings* (both Lark Books, 2006). Her web site is christinedhein. com.

MOLLY DINGLEDINE, a graduate of the Savannah College of Art and Design, creates jewelry in Asheville, North Carolina. Having grown up by the ocean in Charleston, South Carolina, and now living in the mountains of western North Carolina, she feels that her work is continually inspired by the natural forms around her.

JOANNA GOLLBERG is a studio artist working in Asheville, North Carolina. She graduated from the Fashion Institute of Technology with a degree in jewelry design, and exhibits her work at craft fairs and galleries throughout the United States. Gollberg has taught workshops in North Carolina at the Penland School of Crafts and the John C. Campbell Folk School, and she is the author of three books published by Lark Books: *Making Metal Jewelry* (2003), *Creative Metal Crafts* (2004), and *The Art and Craft of Making Jewelry* (2006).

S. RAMSEY HALL lives in Murfreesboro, Tennessee, and she graduated with a BFA degree in metals from that city's Middle Tennessee State University. She creates an original line of jewelry along with one-of-a-kind pieces that she sells at fine craft fairs throughout the southeastern U.S. Her recent work consists of abstract mixed-metal collages made with silver, gold, and copper.

KRISTIN LORA has an extensive corporate background, including an MBA from Cornell, but is now a full-time metalsmith in Santa Fe, New Mexico. When creating her one-of-a-kind jewelry and small sculptures, she strives for bold, contemporary lines and a sense of whimsy. Lora has shown her work at numerous galleries and exhibitions, and she has served on the board of directors of such organizations as New Mexico Women in the Arts and the Society of North American Goldsmiths.

TONYA MOORE is a studio artist working out of her stone cottage located in Asheville, North Carolina. She creates a wide range of contemporary mixed media jewelry focusing on organic shapes, interesting textures, and playful colors. A graduate of the professional craft program at Haywood Community College in western North Carolina and a member of the Society of North American Goldsmiths, Moore has exhibited her work at the Grovewood Gallery in Asheville.

AMY TAVERN is a studio jeweler who has been working with metal since 1998. She graduated from the University of Washington with a BFA in metal design in 2002. She creates one-of-a-kind art jewelry, production-line jewelry, and wedding rings at her studio in Seattle, Washington. Her work can be viewed at www.amytavern.com.

TERRY TAYLOR is an editor and writer in Asheville, North Carolina. His creative work includes jewelry, mixed-media pieces, and a wide variety of craft-projects-on-demand for Lark Books. He has studied jewelry and metalwork at John C. Campbell Folk School, Appalachian Center for Crafts, and Haystack Mountain School of Crafts.

GALLERY ARTISTS INDEX

ACKNOWLEDGMENTS

Thanks to the many talented people at Lark Books who helped produce this book, especially Megan Kirby, Cindy La Breacht, Mark Bloom, Cassie Moore, Dawn Dillingham, and Terry Taylor. Thanks to Patricia Meyerowitz, whose writings on this type of jewelry construction provided inspiration. Thanks to the gallery artists for their creative works. And most of all, thanks to the contributing artists for their inspired designs and helpful text, with a special thanks to those who contributed jewelry components to be photographed.

NOTES ABOUT SUPPLIERS

Usually, the supplies you need for making the projects in Lark books can be found at your local craft supply store, discount mart, home improvement center, or retail shop relevant to the topic of the book. Occasionally, however, you may need to buy materials or tools from specialty suppliers. In order to provide you with the most up-to-date information, we have created a listing of suppliers on our web site, which we update on a regular basis. Visit us at www.larkbooks.com, click on "Craft Supply Sources," and then click on the relevant topic. You will find numerous companies listed with their web address and/or mailing address and phone number.

INDEX